Prayers of Comfort

Marie Jones, Karen Leet, Carol Stigger, Diana Thrift

Publications International, Ltd.

Marie Jones is a widely published writer of articles, books, and essays and is a contributor to many Publications International, Ltd., titles, including *Whispers from Heaven for the Christmas Spirit, How to Let God Help You Through Hard Times,* and *A Mother's Daily Prayer Book.* She is the creator of Gigglebug Farms *Simply Storybook* children's videos.

Karen Leet is a freelance writer who holds an M.A. in modern literature. Her inspirational stories and articles are published by a variety of national publications, including *Christian Reader, Evangel, Sunday Digest,* and *Today's Christian Woman.* She has contributed to several Publications International, Ltd., titles including the magazine *Whispers from Heaven* and the book *Whispers from Heaven for the Christmas Spirit.*

Carol Stigger is a writer specializing in third-world poverty and social justice. Her work has taken her to more than 20 countries, and her articles have been published nationally and internationally in numerous magazines, newspapers, and books, including the Publications International, Ltd., titles *Whispers from Heaven* magazine and *Daily Prayer Book: Prayers for Our Country.*

Diana Thrift is a freelance author and editor who enjoys writing inspirational pieces and personal essays. She has contributed to several Publications International, Ltd., titles including *An Angel by Your Side* and *Whispers from Heaven for the Christmas Spirit.*

Louis Weber, CEO
Publications International, Ltd.
7373 North Cicero Avenue
Lincolnwood, Illinois 60712

Manufactured in U.S.A.

8 7 6 5 4 3 2 1

ISBN: 0-7853-8685-8

Contents

Finding Forgiveness

Be kind to one another, tenderhearted, forgiving one another, as God in Christ has forgiven you.

—EPHESIANS 4:32 NRSV

Heavenly Father, teach me to forgive others their transgressions and to let go of angers and resentments that poison the heart and burden the soul. Teach me to love and understand others and to accept them as they are, not as I wish they would be. Amen.

An apology is a friendship preserver, an antidote for hatred, never a sign of weakness; it costs nothing but one's pride, always saves more than it costs, and is a device needed in every home.

—Author Unknown

The act of forgiveness is promised by God to never go unacknowledged.

Lord God, it is hard for us to accept when someone else hurts us. We don't want to talk to the person anymore. We consider our friendship to be over. And all because our pride is bruised. Please help us to recognize when we are not giving others a chance. Amen.

You are a God ready to forgive.

—NEHEMIAH 9:17 NRSV

The people around me are irritating me, God. With an apology on my lips, help me to climb out of this rut of irritation and make amends. Help me learn from my mistakes and do better. Amen.

The Lord is merciful and gracious,
slow to anger and abounding in
steadfast love.

—Psalm 103:8 NRSV

A Debt Forgiven

Martha Maude invited me to walk downtown with her at lunchtime. She planned to buy a treat at Mr. Kelley's store. I thought my friend knew my financial situation and would buy something for me, too. When she did not, I asked Mr. Kelley if I could charge a candy bar and a soda. When I told him my dad's name, he said my credit was good.

Martha Maude kept inviting me to join her for lunch, so my debt began to increase. I soon found myself three dollars in debt. Mr. Kelley said firmly, "No more credit for you, young lady. You need to pay back what you've spent."

I suddenly realized what I had done. It was not just me who was responsible for the debt—it was my dad's name that was on the line. My father was strict, and I dreaded the punishment I was sure to receive. Desperately, I tried to think of a way to pay off my debt.

My mother noticed that I was unusually quiet when I got home from school that day. She asked me what was wrong. I confessed to her about my debt and how I'd used Dad's name. She said soothingly, "We'll think of something."

After school the next day, Mother instructed me to help Dad dig potatoes. I dragged my feet to the hilltop where he was working. Several feed sacks and one new bushel basket were set

out at the beginning of the freshly plowed rows. Dad showed me how to get the biggest and best-formed potatoes, rub off the dirt, and place them, unbruised, into the basket. *Who is it for?* I wondered. *Probably for some special person.*

At sundown, we loaded my basket and several sacks of smaller potatoes into the wagon and started for home. Dad said, "Your mother tells me you owe Mr. Kelley some money."

Frightened, sad, and sorry, I began to babble. "I'm gonna pay him, Dad. . . . I just need more time. . . . I'll figure something out."

"I don't know how you think you can pay him. Nobody's hiring."

Nervously I blathered on, "I thought maybe I could take him some butter . . . or eggs . . . or maybe sweep out his store. . . . "

"Mr. Kelley told me that a bushel of Irish potatoes will settle your bill. I'll take him that

basket you fixed. But don't you ever buy anything on credit again. Understand?"

"Yes, sir," I whispered, unable to say more.

I learned some important lessons. My father and Mr. Kelley showed me the power of forgiveness. Dad taught me that when I give something away, I should give my best. I also found out how important it is to think before I act, especially when someone else's name is on the line.

Who knew I could get all that from having lunch with Martha Maude?

Lord, teach me to think ahead about the results my actions might inflict. If things go awry despite my forethought, help me admit my wrongs and right them. Amen.

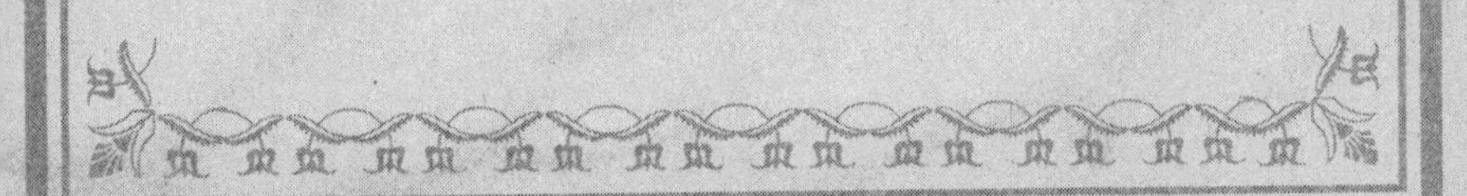

Comfort me in my day of need with a love that is infinite and true. Ignore my lack of desire to forgive and forget. Fill my anger with the waters of peace and serenity that I may come to accept this situation and move on to a greater level of understanding and knowing.

A man should never be ashamed to own he has been in the wrong, which is but saying, in other words, that he is wiser today than he was yesterday.

—JONATHAN SWIFT, *THOUGHTS ON VARIOUS SUBJECTS*

God pardons like a mother who kisses the offense into everlasting forgetfulness.

—Henry Ward Beecher

God, I do not intend to hurt you and others. I am not always sure what happens in those times when I do hurt you and others. I am thankful that you forgive. Please help others to forgive me, too. Remind us all to follow your teachings. We pray that you will guide and comfort us.

My friend and I have had a falling-out, Lord. The atmosphere is strained between us; the air is chilly. I don't know what I've said or done to cause this breach in our relationship. I only know we're both at odds. Relieve the anguish that I feel, Lord. Show me how to break the silence. Help me to take the first step to mend this rift between us, then you can do the rest. Heal us with your love.

Hold on tight to your friends; they are one of God's great blessings.

Bear with each other and forgive whatever grievances you may have against one another. Forgive as the Lord forgave you.

—COLOSSIANS 3:13 NIV

The Better Life

Our divorce, after 18 years of a rocky marriage, brought out the worst in me. As the "wronged woman," I felt I had the right to share with our small gossipy town every one of Ted's mean-spirited words and deeds from our first arguments through the final court date. I lived in the home he had built for us, now all mine. Our mutual friends were now all mine, too. As for the children, he did not try for custody. What

judge would give custody to an alcoholic living with a woman who was known for her wild behavior? I wouldn't even refer to her by her name—instead I called her That Woman.

After eight months, Ted was still finding excuses to visit me. Around the holidays, it was an expired credit card. We both knew he just wanted comfort from me. He apologized for his past actions and asked for forgiveness from me. I handed him his gloves that he had laid hopefully on the foyer table and told him I had nothing left to give. He put his hand on the front doorknob, and the slump of his shoulders shamed me.

It was Advent. When my youngest son lit the first Advent candle at church a few days before, I had vowed that all those who entered my home would leave with more than they brought. I thought my vow would be easy to keep. I did

not consider the fact that Ted might be the test of my faithfulness.

"Wait," I told him. He looked surprised. But the biggest surprise was what I knew I had to give him. It certainly wasn't my nasty, bruised spirit that was telling me to part with such a treasure. I knew if I told him to come back later, I would find a way to talk myself out of it.

"Please sit," I said. "No, don't take off your coat," I added as I went into my room and sat on my bed. I took my Bible from the night-stand. On the first page was a message from my mother who had given me the Bible on my eighth Easter: "Read this wisely, and learn to live the better life."

I took my Bible to Ted. His eyes filled with tears. "Start with the Book of John," I said.

We looked at each other across the Bible and across the years. We looked at each other without rage and without words. He tucked the Bible under his arm and pulled on his gloves. I quietly closed the door behind him.

Would my Bible end up in That Woman's house? Perhaps, but her name was Lynn, and it was time I started calling her that. I had—for the moment at least—forgiven Ted. Maybe I had read that precious book wisely after all. Perhaps I was finally learning to live "the better life."

Heavenly Father, give us the forgiving spirit we so badly need to heal the wounds of the past. Help us to live "the better life" by making peace with our enemies and understanding that they, too, need your love. Amen.

I pray, Lord, for the ability to learn forgiveness. Often within my heart there is much that is negative. I pray to learn to let go of those feelings. I pray to learn to forgive others as I wish to be forgiven. I pray for the gifts of understanding and compassion as I strive to be more like you. Amen.

Judge not, and ye shall not be judged: condemn not, and ye shall not be condemned: forgive, and ye shall be forgiven.

—LUKE 6:37 KJV

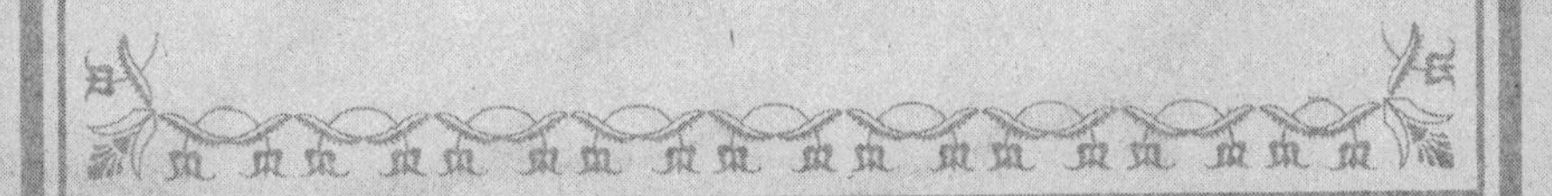

Forgiveness is the first step to spiritual freedom. We cannot truly pray with an open heart if we are filled with malice toward ourselves or others.

Lord above, you look down upon us, and still you love us. When we look down on others, it is because we are angered and cannot see their points of view. We also still love them, but sometimes our anger clouds our love. Please help us to stay grounded and find understanding. Amen.

Therefore confess your sins to one another, and pray for one another, so that you may be healed. The prayer of the righteous is powerful and effective.

—James 5:16 NRSV

Dear God, I know that I have wronged others over the course of the years. I pray that those moments are long forgotten, and if they are not, I pray that I might somehow make them right. I truly forgive anyone who has wronged me, letting go of any grudges or hurtful feelings. And I pray that as I forgive, so may I be forgiven. Amen.

Blessed are the peacemakers, for they will be called children of God.

—Matthew 5:9 NRSV

Julia's Journey Home

Julia always knew that one day the phone call would come. When it did, it was the voice of a stranger who told her, "Your mother is in the hospital. She's had a stroke."

Julia fixed herself a strong cup of tea. She thought about her childhood poisoned by her mother's alcoholism and her father's violence. At 18 she'd moved out and hadn't spoken to her parents in 15 years—she did not even attend her father's funeral. Now her mother was sick, alone, and possibly dying. After years of therapy

dealing with her childhood's legacy of anxiety and depression, Julia finally felt good about life and about herself. She now wanted to forgive her mother and, if possible, mend their broken relationship. She put down her cup of tea and reached for the phone to book a flight.

A week later, accompanied by Rose, her supportive friend, Julia flew to New York City. Although the woman lying in the hospital bed seemed like a stranger, Julia offered to take care of her if she would relocate to Julia's home in Phoenix, Arizona. Her mother gratefully accepted. Julia and Rose set about the task of sorting through her mother's belongings. They would need to get her mother's brownstone home ready to be put on the market.

Nothing could have prepared Julia for the sights and smells that greeted her when she entered her mother's home. Empty bourbon

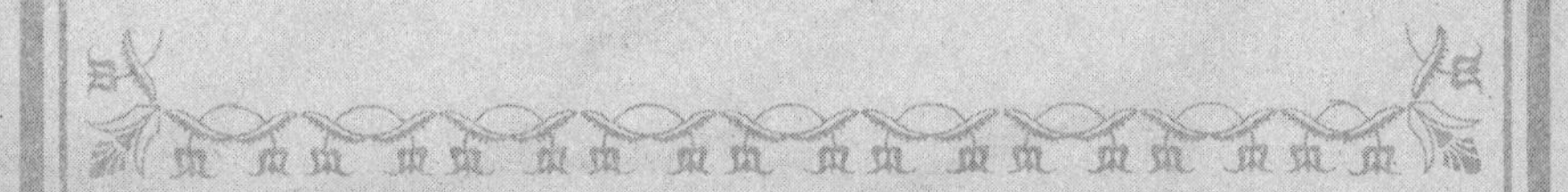

bottles and microwave dinner boxes littered the expensive countertops and tile floors. The odor of cigarettes, dirty dishes, and unwashed clothes hung in the air. The shame Julia felt as a child came flooding back, threatening her resolve to reconcile with her mother. Feeling trapped and afraid, she left Rose in the doorway and fled down the busy city sidewalks.

Several blocks away, Julia saw a small church tucked in between two skyscrapers. Without hesitation, she entered, sat quietly in the back, and began to pray for the strength she needed to forgive herself and her mother. She asked for forgiveness for having stayed away for so long. She asked for forgiveness for not being able to save her mother from either alcoholism or her abusive father.

Physically and emotionally spent, Julia must have dozed, lulled by the gentle peacefulness

that had begun to pervade her heart. She dreamed she saw her mother as a beautiful young woman, graceful and radiant with love, walking toward her. The woman spoke, saying, "Please forgive me," and then disappeared. Suddenly wide awake, Julia realized that the woman in the dream embodied her mother's true essence, before it became veiled by bitterness and alcoholism. She saw that it was not her mother's true essence that she had lived with all those years, but instead a lost, desperate soul. Holding the image of her "real" mother in her heart, Julia touched a place of deep compassion for this woman full of hopes, dreams, and good intentions, this woman destined to be disappointed and hurt by life.

Julia also saw how the pain she experienced in her childhood had sensitized her to the pain and vulnerability of others, how each hurt she sustained could be viewed as a call to deepen her compassion toward others and herself.

Rose was washing dishes when Julia returned. She had aired the place out and bagged most of the trash. She smiled at Julia as though nothing unusual had happened. But as Julia grabbed a dishtowel and reached for a wet plate, she knew she had just begun the most important journey of her life, a journey toward forgiveness and her own true essence: love.

Dear God, help us see that none of us are immune to losing ourselves or to hurting one another. Please help us stay on course so we may find our own true essences. Amen.

Father in heaven, sometimes I feel anger welling up inside me, and I need to turn to you for counsel. Please stay near to me and help me find ways to express my emotions without harming another's feelings or getting myself so upset I cannot see past my own feelings. I need to understand myself, express myself, and accept myself—all within the bounds of your teachings. Amen.

Anger must be expressed, or it turns in on itself. The secret is to express it in ways that are not damaging but are productive.

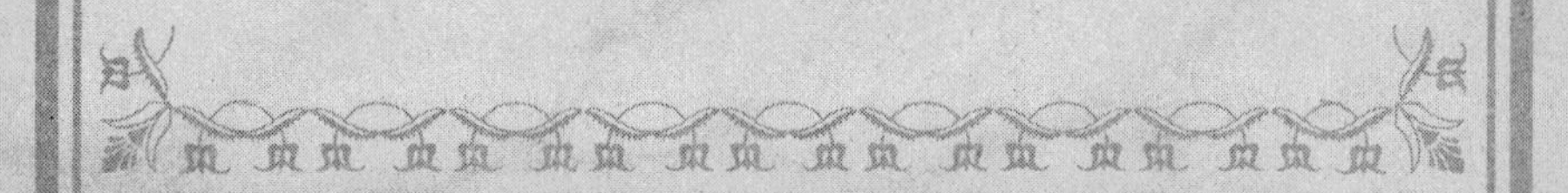

Above all, maintain constant love for one another, since love covers a multitude of sins.

—1 PETER 4:8 NRSV

Lord, your forgiveness, based on your love for me, has transformed my life. I've experienced inner healing and freedom in knowing that you have wiped my slate clean and made me your friend. Help me become an extension of your love to those around me. Let healing happen as I apply the salve to the wounds they inflict on me. Please strengthen me while I carry it out in your name. Amen.

In thankfulness for present mercy, nothing so becomes us as losing sight of past ills.

—Lew Wallace

Dear God, thank you for children who teach us to be open and forgiving. Help us forgive those who hurt us so the pain will not be passed on through the generations. Thank you for forgiving our sins and help us be at peace with our families. Amen.

All this is from God, who reconciled us to himself through Christ, and has given us the ministry of reconciliation; that is, in Christ God was reconciling the world to himself, not counting their trespasses against them, and entrusting the message of reconciliation to us.

—2 Corinthians 5:18–19 NRSV

Dear God, help us understand that forgiveness opens the door to reconciliation. Amen.

Heavenly Father, it is good to remember that everything that lives and breathes is sacred to you. We must never feel superior to any other human being—for we are all precious in your eyes. You have given us life, and we must make the choices that lead to kindness and peace. You created us, but how we live together is up to us. Thank you.

We have been created to love each other, to help each other, and to heal each other. In doing so, we love, help, and heal ourselves.

A Healing Heart

He is a loving, tender hand, full of sympathy and compassion.

—Dwight L. Moody, *Anecdotes and Illustrations*

Call to me and I will answer you.

—JEREMIAH 33:3 NRSV

Father God, we know that to receive the blessings of healing, the heart must be open. But when we are mad, we close off the heart as if it were a prison. Remind us that a heart that is shut cannot receive understanding, acceptance, and renewal. Even though we feel angry, we must keep the heart's door slightly ajar so your grace can enter and fill our darkness with the light of hope.

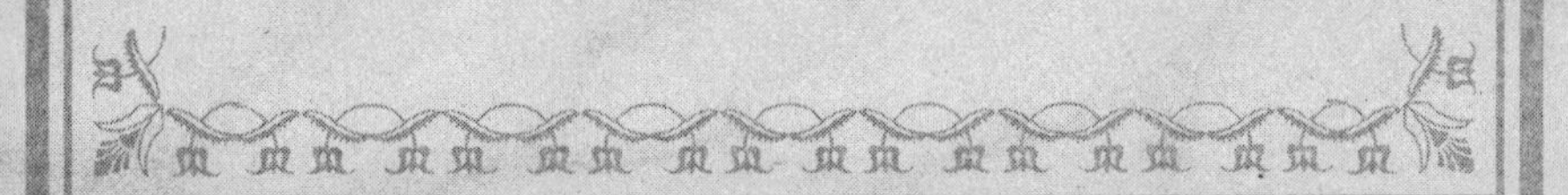

Faith in a wise and trustworthy God, even in broken times like these, teaches us a new math: subtracting old ways and adding new thoughts because sharing with God divides our troubles and multiplies unfathomable possibilities for renewed life.

Dear God, help us to start anew. Teach us how to heal by learning new ways to live. Amen.

Bear one another's burdens.
—GALATIANS 6:2 NRSV

Make a Wish, Mommy

It was my birthday, and I was depressed. In years past, I had celebrated my birthday with my family. But my family was different now. My sister and I had had a falling-out. She had asked me and my two kids to live with her family after my husband died. I would have none of that, though. I was too proud. Didn't she know I could take care of myself? When I had not accepted her invitation, she was angry and offended.

And because I didn't want looks of sympathy to follow me wherever I went in our small

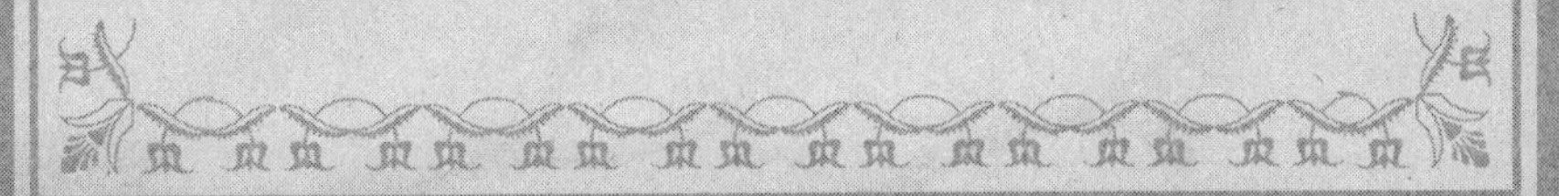

town, I moved to Utah. It was January, and the piles of snow were thigh-high. It was a daily struggle to leave the house, which added to my isolation. It was a winter of loneliness for me.

The day before my birthday, I was a grouch, thinking about how awful my birthday was bound to be—without my husband, my sister, her family, and even presents and a cake. I did not realize just how comfortable I'd gotten with feeling sorry for myself. Tucking the children into bed that night, my mood was a cloud of hopelessness.

The next morning, I got up and began making breakfast. In the adjoining tiny living room, I could hear Nick talking to his younger sister, Maya. He was sternly telling her to make Mommy smile today.

It suddenly hit me. Being so wrapped up in my misery, I hadn't noticed how it was affecting

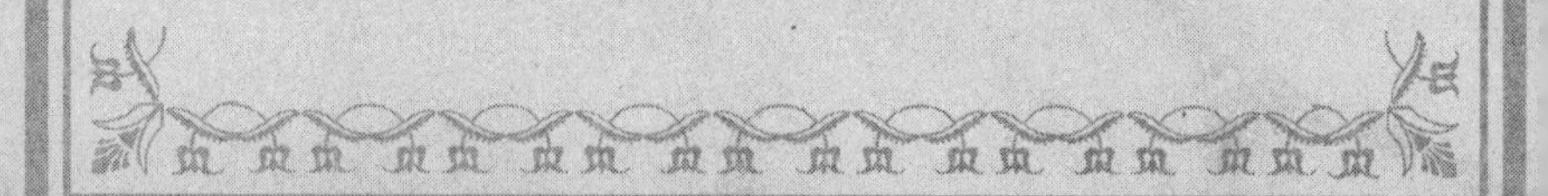

my children. Even my little boy could sense that I wasn't happy, and he was doing his best to make me feel better. Tears of shame at my selfishness welled up in my eyes. I knelt down in our little kitchen and asked for the strength to somehow find happiness again. I asked God to help me *really* see the blessings I had in my life.

I marched into the living room with a smile on my face. Nick and Maya were sitting on the floor with a pile of presents in front of them.

"I surprised you, Mommy, didn't I? Happy birthday!" Nick grinned his toothless grin.

Stunned, I asked him how he had found a way to get me gifts. He reminded me of our trip to the All a Dollar store. I suddenly remembered that I had almost chided him for spending everything he had so carefully saved, but then I had thought better of it and had done my shopping while he had done his.

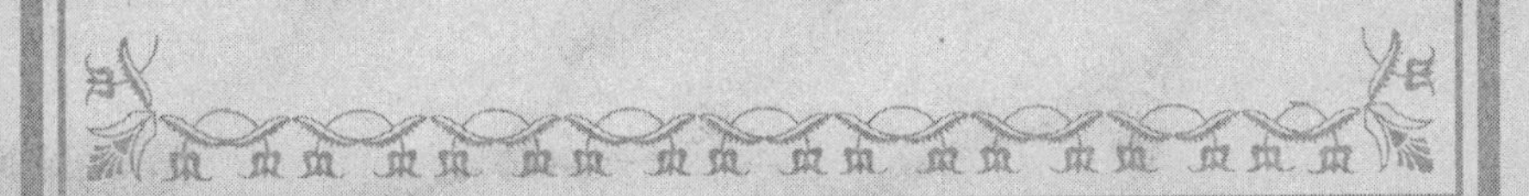

Looking again at the beautiful pile of presents in front of me, I could hardly believe my son had spent everything he had on me.

There, I heard the voice in my heart say, *I am showing you your blessings.* My prayers had definitely been answered. Even my son knew that I needed a little help from other people in order for me to remember my happiness and my blessings.

I opened the last gift, a wax birthday cake, and Nick sang "Happy Birthday" to me. Then Nick said, "Make a wish, Mommy."

That wish was granted because the very next day we headed back home.

Lord, help us not to be stubborn. We want our broken hearts to heal. Amen.

What happiness there is for you who weep, for the time will come when you shall laugh with joy!

—LUKE 6:21 TLB

My Creator, I know in my heart that these tears will one day give way again to joy, yet for now I know only pain. Help me to find the courage to let these tears flow, to feel the loss and heartbreak, so that I may come out whole and cleansed again. For on the other side of my sorrow I know life waits for me. I want to laugh again.

I am like two halves of a walnut, God. I am of two minds: despairing and hopeful. Help me feel your hand holding me together as I rebuild my life when at first it seemed too hard to even try. In order to get to the meat of a walnut, it must be split into halves. May the brokenness I feel get me to the nourishment—the meat—I need in order to move on. Amen.

God's love for us is complete and constant.

Do not let your hearts be troubled.
Believe in God, believe also in me.

—JOHN 14:1 NRSV

Dear Father God, you sent your son to us to be our Lord, to watch over us, to bring us comfort, strength, hope, and healing when our hearts are broken and our lives seem shattered. We will never be alone, not when you are here with us always and forever. Remind us to look to you for strength. Amen.

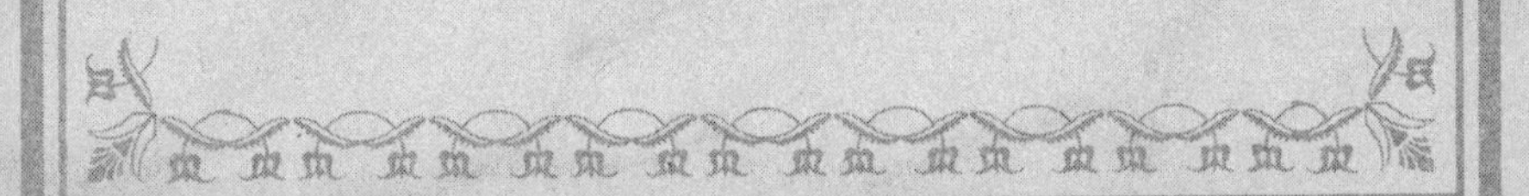

Father, make me resilient like the sandy beach upon which the waves crash. Make me strong like the mighty willow tree that bends but does not break in the high winds. Give me the patience and wisdom to know that my suffering will one day turn to a greater understanding of your ways, your works, and your wonders.

Let suffering swell and subside on its own, like the natural rhythm of the ocean waves upon the steadfast shore.

The Ones You Love

When you take marriage vows, you imagine them to be a lasting pact between two people to always love each other, for better or for worse, in sickness and in health, until death do you part. But then these heartfelt vows have to stand up to the realities of life. I was getting ready to ask Geoff, my husband of ten years, for a divorce.

In retrospect, I thought marriage had been a mistake from the beginning. We had married very young because I was ready to have children. So we got married and had three wonderful children who were to become our whole lives. But, they *were* our whole lives, and Geoff and I filled our days with activities revolving around them to avoid our own marriage's emptiness.

I did love Geoff, but it was more of a companion kind of love; any romance that I had felt at the beginning had dissipated. I thought I had never been in love with him as much as he had been—and was—with me. Still, he was a great father and was always there for me, supporting me throughout our years together.

I knew this was not a decision I could—or should—make on my own, so I prayed each night, asking God to give me the wisdom to handle the situation properly.

When I asked Geoff to talk with me one night, I saw a twinge of panic and pain in his eyes. We discussed the kids, our relationship, everything, and it was then I took a deep breath and told him that I wanted to leave the marriage and would share custody with him equally. I did not want a mean divorce. We had always been friends. I hoped we could remain so.

Geoff begged me to stay with him for the kids' sake. But it was for their sakes, I reasoned, that I needed to be true to my feelings. The conversation did not go as I had hoped. But we compromised and I agreed to move some of my belongings into the guest room, which was a small step toward my sought-after freedom.

I questioned our relationship for months after our first conversation. I felt that I desperately needed to decide one way or another if I should stay with Geoff. And, any time I brought up the subject of divorce, Geoff put me off.

Sometimes, though, I was thankful to still be part of the family. As holidays passed, I found myself grateful for each one. *Even though I know this will be our last one together,* I thought.

God worked slowly but surely. His first lesson: In order for me to be happy, I had to do what was best for everyone involved. Next, I

realized that I had to act from love, not selfishness. That changed my prayers significantly.

I'm not sure when I realized that I no longer wanted to leave. I started to understand that the freedom I thought I needed was really freedom from my illusions that something better was waiting for me. Here I had a man who supported me, loved me, and had fought to keep me a part of our family. Really, could there be anything more romantic?

I moved back into our room. I fell back in love with Geoff—truly—and I started my new life with an appreciation of all that family means.

Dear Father, help me to see that I sometimes amplify bad times because I push others away and become selfish. Please teach me to love. Amen.

Love is patient; love is kind; . . . It does not insist on its own way.

—1 CORINTHIANS 13:4–5 NRSV

God, sometimes I wish I could be saved from the struggle and pain of learning the hard way. But, Lord, that's not your plan, and I need to be willing to wait as you work gently from the inside out. Please grant me some strength in this time of uncertainty. I trust and love you. Amen.

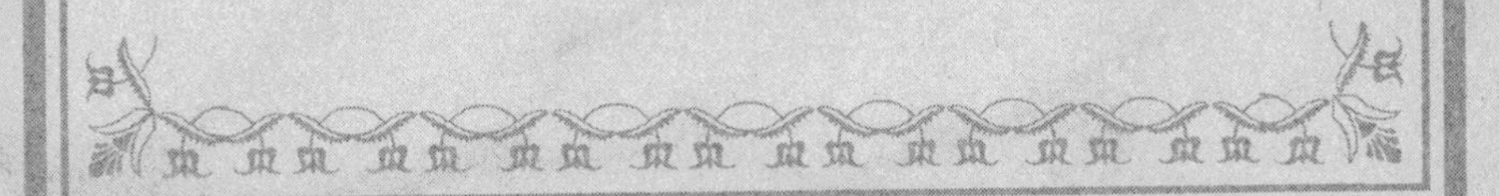

In the dark sea of my despair, dear God, I am afraid, lost, and alone. But I will not give up hope. I will cast out my heart one more time into the deep waters and await your loving salvation. I know you will not fail to lift me up from my sorrow and gently deposit me upon the shore. And though my body is tired and my spirit is weary from weeping, I offer myself to you in complete surrender, so that you may fill my nets with the bounty of your eternal peace and the comfort of your infinite love.

Esau ran to meet [his estranged brother, Jacob], and embraced him, and fell on his neck and kissed him, and they wept.

—Genesis 33:4 NRSV

Lord, I want to leave the fighting behind us. It's time to begin the healing process. Show me how to reconcile and how to be humble without being a doormat. I want the respect we have had for one another to remain intact. Amen.

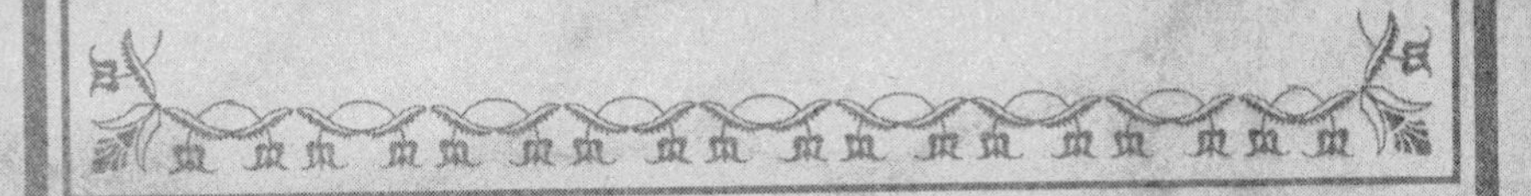

A Break in the Chain

Sometimes a business partnership can be as complicated and intense as any marriage. This is especially true when the partnership is between two best friends. I had decided to go into business with my friend, Janice. We both had a knack for making unique jewelry.

Janice and I had never worked together before. Our different styles became immediately apparent. I wanted to keep the company small, and Janice wanted to go big, to expand and hire as many people to help as we could.

At one point, we signed a deal with a home shopping channel. I knew we could not handle the demand without hiring, and I gave in. Janice found us office space and a warehouse. I wanted

little to do with it. My home-based dream had become a mighty, unwieldy monster.

We sold more jewelry that first month than we did all the previous year. The money was great, but I was now working more than 80 hours a week and I wasn't enjoying it.

After one very exhausting day of meetings, I went into Janice's office. I told her the business no longer satisfied me and had become something I did not want. I suggested that she buy me out and continue running the company, as it was what she did well. I could stay on as a consultant and designer.

I expected Janice would be dismayed, but her reaction shocked me. She told me that since I was not a team player, she would prefer to have me off the team completely. She would buy me out, but only under the condition that I had nothing to do with the company from then on.

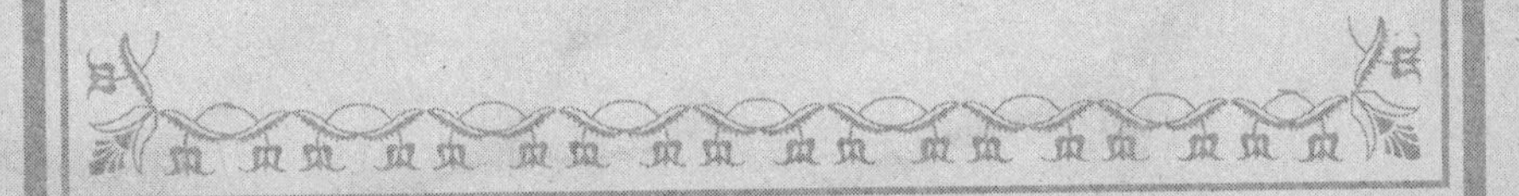

Her cruel reaction sent me reeling down the hallway. I closed my office door and sat for a moment, not sure why I had just been dismissed so abruptly. Then I packed my belongings and left for good.

That night, I cried. Splitting up with a business partner felt just as painful as any divorce. I was not only losing my dreams, but also my best friend. I prayed to God for comfort and peace, and I prayed that Janice would one day realize how much our friendship had meant.

As I prayed, I felt a growing sense of relief and certainty. From now on, I vowed, I was going to let God direct my path. But it still hurt. I didn't know if Janice and I could ever patch up our friendship. I hoped someday we would try.

I followed the company's progress after that, and Janice continued to run a successful ship. I suspected that the business was making Janice

happy. With prayer, I came to accept this. I moved on, too, forming my own small Internet business selling my jewelry creations. I actually turned a profit, and I was enjoying myself again.

I missed Janice, but I was finally living my life and following the dreams God meant just for me. I knew, with time, Janice and I would learn to be friends again. I also knew that God would let me know when the time was right for that to happen.

Dear Lord, when I am sad, you give me hope. When I am lost, you offer me direction and guidance. When I am alone, you stand beside me. When my heart aches with sorrow, you bring me new blessings. Thank you for your gifts of grace, of love, and of healing. Amen.

God is love, and those who abide in love abide in God, and God abides in them....those who love God must love their brothers and sisters also.

—1 John 4:16, 21 NRSV

When I think about your example of love, dear God, I realize that love is far more than a warm emotion. It is a deep commitment to look out for another's best interest, even at my own expense. Please teach me to put my pride and my heart on the line. Please protect me, Lord, as I love others in your name. Amen.

How else but through a broken heart
May Lord Christ enter in?
—OSCAR WILDE, "THE BALLAD OF READING GAOL"

Lord Christ, although the wound seems exposed and open, I understand it must be so for you to cleanse and bandage me. Amen.

Change is a natural process. Without change, nothing can grow.

Everything around me keeps changing, Lord. Nothing lasts. My relationships with others are different than they were before. I started to feel as if there is nothing sure and steady on which I can depend. Then I remembered your ever-present, unchanging love. Through these transitions, your love gives me courage and hope for the future.

The Lord will guide you continually, and satisfy your needs in parched places, and make your bones strong; and you shall be like a watered garden, like a spring of water, whose waters never fail.

—ISAIAH 58:11 NRSV

God, let this sorrow wash over me like cleansing water. Let it rush over my rough-hewn heart and turn me into a smooth and polished stone glistening in the sun. Amen.

Escape from Pain

If you could see through God's eyes, you would see God, seeing you through.

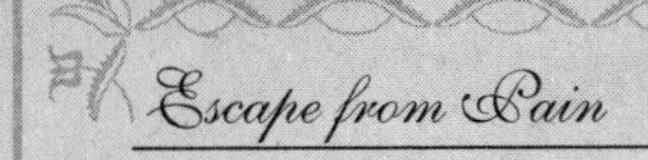

Look upon mine affliction and my pain.

—Psalm 25:18 KJV

When each heartbeat hurts and each breath aches, I pray, God, that you will take some of my blinding pain away. Lift me out of my pain, and give me peace. Amen.

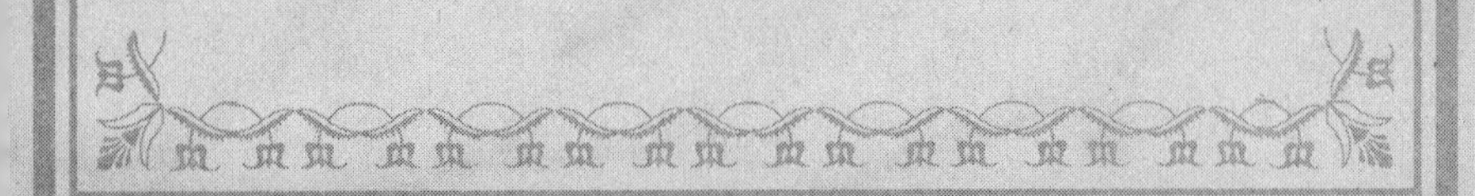

Lord, you do not leave us to suffer alone. You are with us in pain, in sickness, and in our worst moments. Thank you for your comfort and healing power. Thank you for getting us through when our bodies fail, when our health falters, and when we need you most of all. Amen.

Daughter, your faith has made you well; go in peace, and be healed.

—Mark 5:34 NRSV

O God, I know you will never give us a burden to bear without giving us the grace to endure it, but some burdens just seem so heavy we find ourselves wondering if they can be survived. I ask that you send an abundant amount of strength and grace to all those who suffer so. Let them feel your presence in a very real way, Lord, for without you, they have no hope. I ask this in Jesus' name. Amen.

Pray your prayers, then stand back and watch God work.

I'm Paralyzed, But My Spirituality Isn't

In 1993 I dove into a lake and became an instant quadriplegic. I was 14 at the time. And to adapt to this new body and life was the hardest thing I've ever done.

About a week after my accident, I received a poster from a friend. It showed a picture of a blue sky with a dove in flight. And it read: "We cannot change yesterday, but we can change what lies ahead." I loved that poster. My mom taped it to the ceiling over my hospital bed so it was easy for me to see.

After months of physical therapy, I went home. My new life as a person with a disability began. I finished high school, made new friends,

and reorganized what was important to me. I got used to being in a wheelchair instead of walking. As the years passed, I began to think less and less about being paralyzed.

Right after the accident, I prayed a lot. I asked God to heal me, to make me walk again; I specifically prayed that he'd heal me in the middle of the night. I wanted to be able to walk upstairs to my mom's bedroom and surprise her. But that never happened.

Since God wouldn't answer my prayers, I finally stopped praying. Even so, many people told me that I could turn to God for help. But I didn't believe them, and I got sick of hearing about God and how he had a purpose for me. I decided I could take care of myself.

Over the next few years, I continued to feel better, move on, and adjust to my life. I went to a private college where I did well in my classes, I

learned how to drive an adapted van, and I even had a boyfriend who didn't care that I was in a wheelchair. But nearly eight years after the accident, I began to have more moments of pure sadness. I thought I had come to terms with my disability and could live happily ever after for the rest of my life. But jealousy and self-pity were clouding my mind. At first, I figured it was just a down time in my life. But the feelings didn't go away.

Then I remembered what that poster said: "We cannot change yesterday, but we can change what lies ahead." I knew I had to take charge of my future, but I realized I didn't have to handle everything on my own. I could get help. And luckily God was waiting patiently for me to ask him.

I understood then that it was God who had inspired the poster's author to write those mov-

ing words. It was God who had given me strength and courage to make it through my ordeals and transitions. I am still not walking, but I am living. And I am very happy to be here.

God did answer my prayers. He showed me ways to survive, and he was the one who comforted me when I was in doubt. He was there all along, guiding me up that giant hill of life. I just hadn't noticed he was there.

God, it's so hard to see your will while I'm suffering. But while I can't understand your ways, Lord, I trust your heart. Amen.

Blessed be the God and Father of our Lord Jesus Christ..., who consoles us in our affliction.

—2 CORINTHIANS 1:3–4 NRSV

Lord, I am now in tribulation, and my heart is ill at ease, for I am much troubled with the present suffering.... Grant me patience, O Lord, even now in this moment. Help me, my God, and then I will not fear, how grievously soever I be afflicted.

—THOMAS À KEMPIS

To you they cried, and were saved; in you they trusted.

—Psalm 22:5 NRSV

Dear God, I am scared. I hear the doctor's approaching footsteps, but I do not know what news the doctor brings. Please help me use my fear that it may become energy to live more fully, with more appreciation, from this day on. Amen.

Dearest God, my body is slowing, and I am in need of healing. I am scared of illness and of what lies ahead. I ask now for your healing light to shine upon me and favor me with your grace. I ask now for your love. I give myself to you, God, and I pray that you will help me and heal me.

God knows what is best for us, and we are healed accordingly.

Rejoice in hope, be patient in suffering, persevere in prayer.

—Romans 12:12 NRSV

A Friend of Job's Becomes a Friend of Mine

After four months of illness, I was frightened. Three doctors had been unable to diagnose my problem, much less treat it. The Great Physician was not stepping up to the plate either. For three days I would be functional, able to go to work and attend to household chores. Every fourth day I was so stricken with exhaustion, nausea, and pain, I could barely get out of bed. My office was becoming suspicious of my frequent sick days.

I thought I was dying, so I bought a small house in my son's neighborhood. It was comforting to be close to family, but if I didn't get well soon I would be living with them, not down the street.

On my "down" days, I read. When I was nearly finished with *War and Peace,* my son said: "You used to say 'what would Jesus do?' when I was facing problems."

I glared at him. "I read the gospels the first month I was sick. Would you please check out the library's complete works of Dostoyevsky? I vowed I would read all the Russian novels I avoided in college if I were ever bedridden."

"Job is your man this time," he said. He handed me my Bible and left.

I turned to the Book of Job. After his long lament, I discovered a section that was new to me. To paraphrase Job's friend Eliphaz:

I hope I don't make you angry, but don't you remember the friends you encouraged when they were sick or grieving? You told them how to get through it. Now it's your turn, and you are impatient. Your faith is unraveling. Have you forgotten that God will give you confidence? Do you not realize that the truth you spoke to others is your own hope?

I felt that Eliphaz had jumped out of the Bible and was shaking me. I propped my laptop computer on a pillow, turned it on, and opened my "letters" folder. I read my letters to a friend who has AIDS; letters to a friend throughout her cancer diagnosis, treatment, and recovery; letters to an uncle whose brilliant mind is being erased by Alzheimer's. I read those letters as if they were addressed to me.

Although wrapped in different words, the main message was that God was the source of all comfort and healing. I was deeply ashamed that the words of hope I had given to others had meant so little to me when I was the victim.

Two months later, I was still bedridden every fourth day, but my attitude was changing from fear to acceptance. Then, one day—a fourth day—I reached for the phone to call in sick. But I was not tired, nauseated, or in pain. I went to work. I expected to be stricken at any moment, but I made it through the day. Now, two years later, my illness has not returned. But trials and tests of faith loom around every corner. That's why God sends friends like Eliphaz.

God, thank you for letting me cling to the faith that has sustained me through so much uncertainty and pain before. I now know that although faith may be all I have, it's also all I need.

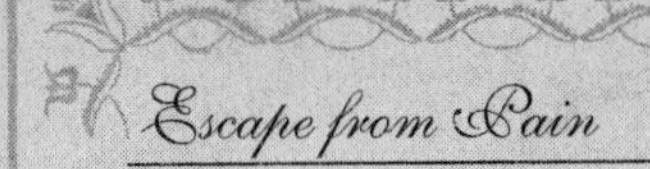

A cheerful heart is a good medicine, but a downcast spirit dries up the bones.

—Proverbs 17:22 NRSV

Father, instill in me the gifts of humor and joy. Teach me how to lift downcast spirits and dispense the medicine of good cheer in your name.

Humor is proof of humanity's ability to overcome adversity.

I called to the Lord out of my distress, and he answered me; out of the belly of Sheol I cried, and you heard my voice.

—JONAH 2:2 NRSV

I cry out to you, O Lord, from the belly of my fear. In this dark pit of anxiety and confusion over my health, I ask that you reach in and guide me into the light of day. My faith in you is strong, and my trust in you is steadfast. Come to my aid, O Lord, as you did when Jonah called to you. Amen.

So we do not lose heart. Even though our outer nature is wasting away, our inner nature is being renewed day by day.

—2 Corinthians 4:16 NRSV

Heavenly Father, help us examine every passing day in order to find purpose in our lives. We want our time to be worthwhile. Remind us to count all our blessings, big and small. Amen.

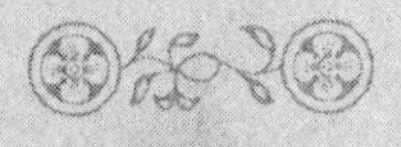

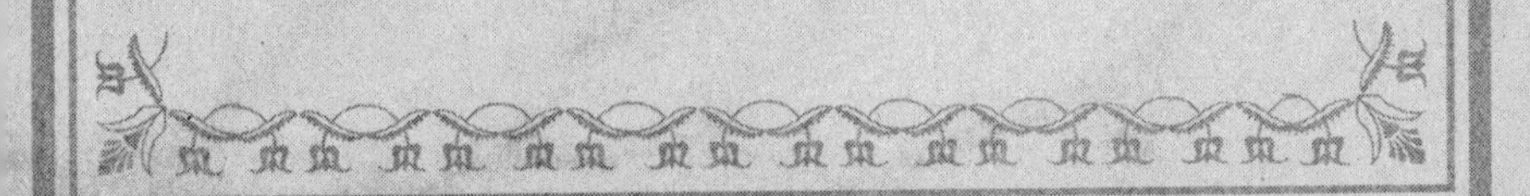

O Father, I feel my heart panic. I am so afraid because my world seems to be in such horrible jeopardy. Help me turn to you for courage during this dreadful time. Increase my faith and strengthen my confidence in your care for my welfare. This, I pray. Amen.

Do not be afraid of sudden panic...for the Lord will be your confidence.

—Proverbs 3:25–26 NRSV

Burning Hot

Sarah held her two-year-old son Ben close to her, feeling the heat pouring from him, almost burning into her flesh. Rocking back and forth in her old wooden rocker, Sarah hummed softly to soothe him back to sleep as he thrashed and fussed. It was too soon for more medicine. He felt so hot, way too hot. She didn't know what to do; she didn't know how to help him.

Watching her beloved son suffer was far more difficult than suffering herself. He was too young to understand what was happening to him. His feverish eyes opened to stare at her. He looked dazed, not quite awake.

Sarah dabbed a cool, wet cloth on his face and arms to try to lower the fever. Should she

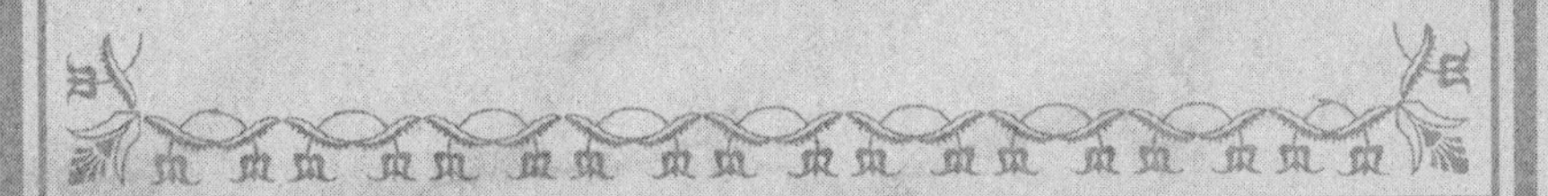

call the doctor again? She felt so worried and so helpless to take away Ben's pain. She wanted to do something to make it better.

But the doctor had given her instructions, had told her small children got fevers, had said that the medication would help, and had asked that she call in the morning if she had questions. She couldn't bring herself to call him again.

So, she rocked Ben and wiped sweaty hair back off his forehead. She counted the minutes until he could take another dose of the medicine. The whole time she wished she could absorb his pain and take it into her own flesh.

His pain was hers in a way already. She felt it because his hot little body was against her own. When he woke, she told him silly stories and sang gentle songs to quiet him. When he dozed fitfully, she prayed over him, yearning for the

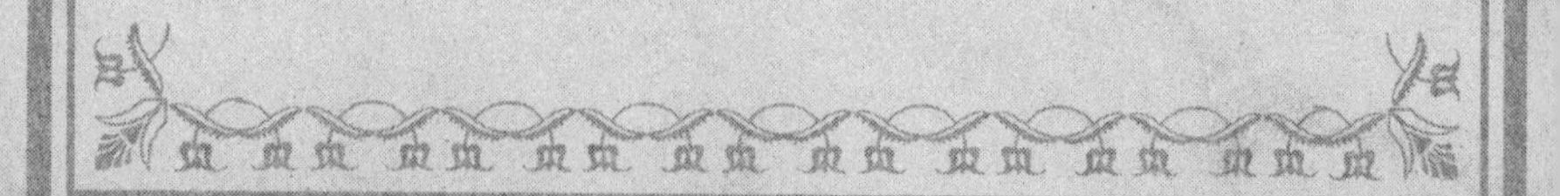

fever to break. The night crept along, endlessly, slowly moving toward dawn.

The doctor wasn't even sure what caused the fever. A cold was the possible culprit. Or it could have happened just because of one of those odd baby ailments that came on suddenly and vanished just as quickly. Why wouldn't this one disappear? She wished and prayed for it to go away and leave her son alone. Then, suddenly, he thrashed harder in her arms, flailing against her and crying out with pain.

Sarah bent over her son, praying fiercely, fighting the fear that rose in her. What if he was worse? What if the fever had shot even higher? What if this was some terrible, fatal disease the doctor hadn't recognized?

Ben felt so hot, as if he were burning up from the inside out. Sarah cried out in her heart to God for help for her precious, little son. It was then that an incredible peace spread through her. Ben quieted. Perhaps he felt it, too. Curled together in the rocker, both slept. Hours later, when Sarah woke, still cradling her son against her body, she could tell at once the fever had broken. He felt cooler. His color looked better. He slept peacefully, his little body relaxed and at ease. She slipped him into his own bed and dozed beside him in the rocker. As he slept, she wept with gratitude.

That next morning, Ben climbed from his bed, full of energy as usual, strong and sturdy. It was as if he'd never been sick and in pain at all.

Please be with us, Lord, when pain strikes us or those we love. Please watch over us when our bodies are stricken. Amen and amen.

God, I hold fast to you at this present moment, for it is the only way for me to have perspective and hope for life beyond this pain I have. And yet, come quickly for I am tired. Fill me with your strength for I feel weak. Add meaning to these days of pain, and finally call me to a new day when I can serve you with a renewed purpose and passion. Amen.

After troubles recede, remember to continue to pray.

God, help us see beyond our pain. We trust and love you. Amen.

This short time of distress will result in God's richest blessing upon us forever and ever! So we do not look at what we can see right now, the troubles all around us, but we look forward to the joys in heaven which we have not yet seen.

—2 Corinthians 4:17–18 TLB

Finally, be strong in the Lord and in the strength of his power.

—EPHESIANS 6:10 NRSV

Lord, please be my strength. When I am scared, please make me brave. When I am unsteady, please bring your stability to me. I look to your power for an escape from the pain. I welcome your comfort. Amen.

Peace Be with You

*W*hen the cares of my heart are many,
your consolations cheer my soul.
—PSALM 94:19 NRSV

Don't worry about anything; instead, pray about everything; tell God your needs and don't forget to thank him for the answers. If you do this you will experience God's peace, which is far more wonderful than the human mind can understand. His peace will keep your thoughts and your hearts quiet.

—PHILIPPIANS 4:6–7 TLB

Lord, I pray I can find a place within my heart where I can let go of worries. I want to be filled with the calmness of a faith in you. Amen.

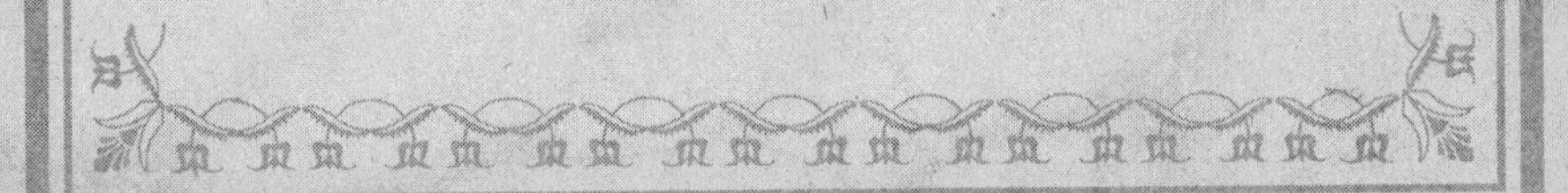

When they call to me, I will answer them.

—Psalm 91:15 NRSV

Confusion is directing my thoughts. My mind loyally follows its erratic demands and becomes increasingly lost and frustrated. I need a sign to orient myself and to find my way out of this turmoil. Find me, Lord, for I am wandering in the wilderness of my own mind, heading deeper and deeper into despair. Where are you? *I call. And then I realize that by describing my lostness, you show me where I am and how to return home.*

*P*eace I leave with you; my peace I give to you. . . . Do not let your hearts be troubled, and do not let them be afraid.

—JOHN 14:27 NRSV

Happy Birthday to Me

*M*y anxiety had been growing as my impending 40th birthday confronted me with my own mortality. At 40, my mother had lost her battle with breast cancer, and my doctor suggested my own risk might be high. He recommended a test that would show if I had reason to worry, but I was worried enough without any test.

I worried through sleepless nights. I berated myself for my moodiness, but I couldn't seem to shake the feeling that the world was an unfriendly place and that life was a burden that had to be suffered through.

Recently, my friend Cathy told me I ought to see someone to talk things over. I just shook my head. Then yesterday in my mailbox was an envelope with a brochure from a spiritual retreat in the nearby New Mexico mountains. There was also a card that said:

Megan,

My birthday present to you is a cottage at this place reserved in your name for this weekend.

Love,

Cathy

She shouldn't have wasted the money, I thought as I crumpled the brochure. Then, I slowly smoothed it out as a little voice in my head whispered, *Why not? What is there to lose?*

The next morning, I threw a suitcase in my car, all the while fighting the urge to just forget

the whole retreat. I drove into the mountains toward the old mission that served as the retreat. A man in a brown robe showed me to a one-room cottage surrounded by scrub trees. "Meals are taken in the dining room with the few other guests," he said, "but talking is not encouraged unless one wants to meet with a spiritual advisor."

"I wasn't planning on that," I said. "Just hoping for a good night's sleep."

"Peace," he said, smiling.

There was a Bible and a flashlight on the table in the sparsely furnished room and a rustic wooden cross on the wall. I closed the curtains and stretched out on the bed. I awoke briefly at the dinner bell, but rolled over and ignored it. *A missed meal couldn't hurt, especially considering the kind of gruel they probably serve up here,* I thought as I fell into a deep sleep.

At midnight, something woke me again. I fumbled for the flashlight, couldn't find it, grabbed the Bible instead, and stepped outside. The sight that greeted me was beautiful and surreal like an artist's canvas: brilliant stars painted boldly bright and a thin crescent moon that glowed as if lit from within. I walked to a wooden bench. A coyote howled and another answered until their voices rose in a cacophonous tribute to the night, to the stark mountains, and to the creator of this perfect beauty.

Looking at the mountains, at the enormous sky, and at the stars that were light-years away in a vast universe, I felt a peacefulness wash over me, and my own problems no longer seemed insurmountable. I realized that with help I could face whatever would come. I would have the test, and if it showed a higher risk, I'd be better off to know early, and if it showed no increased risk, I would have a weight lifted. And either way I could get on with my life.

In this crystalline chapel of earth and sky, I asked God to help me hold on to this peace I'd found. Tomorrow I would talk to a spiritual advisor, and when I got home, I would call Cathy to thank her for this incredible gift.

Our worries are hard to dismiss, Lord. They seem to grow bigger and bigger until they take over our lives. Please help us conquer them, one at a time. Your reassurance is welcome. Amen.

May I have a moment to speak with you, O God? I know there is so much going on in the world that requires your attention. It's just that sometimes I feel tension getting a grip on me and worry clouds my view. This distances me from you and from everything in my life. I pray for the freedom to worry less. I want to simply trust you more.

Faith is the foundation upon which a happy, healthy life is built. The stronger our faith, the less our life can be shaken by outside occurrences and extraneous circumstances.

With weeping they shall come, and with consolations I will lead them back, I will let them walk by brooks of water, in a straight path in which they shall not stumble.

—Jeremiah 31:9 NRSV

Heavenly Father, our diversions seem great. We can't remember when the insurmountable demands started piling up, and we have a hard time seeing the end. Allow us to take a moment from our hectic days to close our eyes and feel your peace. We ask you to lead us. Amen.

Mental illness can be so devastating, Lord. Few understand the heartaches involved in diseases that carry no apparent physical scars. Be with those friends, neighbors, and family members who deal daily with difficult situations of which we are often unaware. Touch them with your special love, and let them know that they can lean on you, Lord. Ease their burdens, quell their sadness, and calm their desperation. Bring peace and healing to these households.

Sometimes I feel abandoned, Lord. I feel empty inside, and it's hard to connect with myself, with others, and with the world. I almost lose faith at these times, Lord. Please stay with me and help me remember your love, your light, and your peace.

Let us know the truth of thy promise: that the whole world may not be able to take away thy peace.

—Søren Kierkegaard

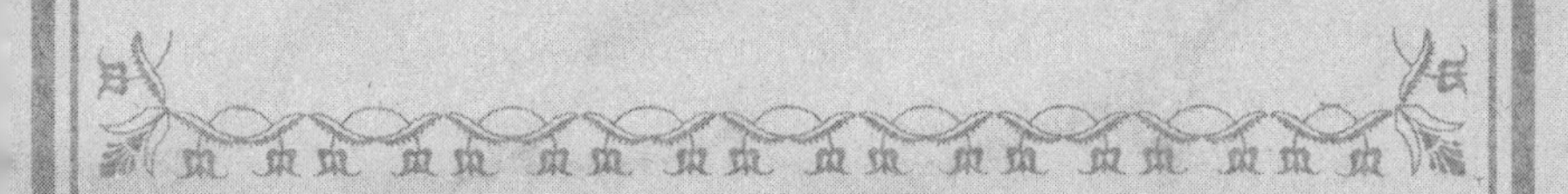

Though we may not think there is something to gain in the depths of despair, it is only when we begin to heal that we finally see the truth.

Lord, help me to recover my lost self. I have been sad for so long that I cannot even begin to think about a good life. Help me find acceptance. Help me cope with nightmares that threaten to begin my despair all over again. Give me the strength to get through each coming day a little more intact. Fill me with the hope of a new dawn that I may see the sunrise once again. Amen.

My brothers and sisters, whenever you face trials of any kind, consider it nothing but joy, because you know that the testing of your faith produces endurance; and let endurance have its full effect, so that you may be mature and complete, lacking in nothing.

—JAMES 1:2–4 NRSV

Gray Days

Every day felt gray and dreary. Nothing felt good. I could barely drag myself out of bed every day, dreading the chores ahead of me.

Financial troubles had piled up. I was hardly managing to pay the bills—no way to be sure they'd be paid next month, though. I couldn't

find a full-time job, so I struggled to hold down several part-time jobs, as well as take care of laundry, meals, the house, and the kids. I felt swamped every single moment of every day.

I laughed out loud at TV talk shows when they advised making time for yourself in a busy schedule. I thought, *Sure, right, when would that be? Instead of sleeping?*

I knew I was depressed. But I didn't know what could I do about it. I didn't have time, energy, or money for medication or doctors. If I thought about the depression, I considered it one more obstacle to climb over each day. It also seemed like my attention was diverted frequently, and none of these demands were any good. The kids even had problems at school.

I felt I was spread so thin you could see through me the way you could see through the knees of my son's worn-out jeans. I forced my-

self to keep going, although all I wanted to do was crawl under the covers and hide my head.

I believed in God, but he seemed to be very busy elsewhere. I prayed but still felt frantic, stressed, and anxious. Where was God when I needed him?

"God, I need time off," I whispered late one night, surrounded by bills I hadn't figured out how I was going to pay. "I need time to myself, time to regain strength. Help, please."

This time felt different. It felt like God had heard and cared. I didn't feel as alone. In fact, I noticed a quiet peace creep through me. The next morning, the sun came out, as if a special gift just for me. Unexpected money showed up in the mail. The kids were invited to friends' houses, and I had the house to myself.

His peace settled more fully over me. I soaked it up, enjoying the silence in my home,

seeing flowers starting to bud in the yard, and finding a good book I'd meant to read months ago. I felt refreshed and renewed. That energy continued to flow through me. I cleaned closets, just for fun. I sewed new covers for the sofa throw pillows to brighten the living room. I cooked three new meals each week. I tried out hairstyles and put together new outfits. And I thanked God for his gift of peace, for his presence, and for the new hope I felt knowing that he was near, that he heard my cries, and that he sent an answer to my prayers.

Dear God, please send your peace to calm us when we're overwhelmed. Your presence wipes away depression and despair. It renews our hope and lifts our hearts. Amen.

When the road into the future looms endlessly dark, remember ancient desert nomads who only traveled in the dark because of the heat during the day. They sewed tiny candleholders on their shoes so they always had enough light for the next step.

We are blinded by our sorrow. Lift our eyes and bless us, O Father, with a defiant hope, steadfast trust, and fire in the belly to emerge from this darkness victorious and whole once again, standing in the light you've given us.

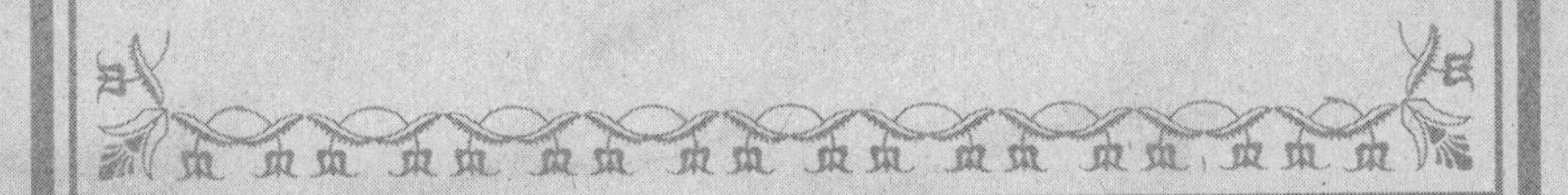

Lord, we confess that our thoughts and beliefs can act as our outstretched wings or prison bars. Save us from the downward spiral where we think defeating thoughts, become depressed, and then act in hopeless ways. Break the cycle, O Lord! Set us free from ideas that imprison our minds and shackle our actions. Restore us to balance so we may soar through the peaks and the valleys with outstretched wings. Amen.

O that I had wings like a dove! I would fly away and be at rest.

—Psalm 55:6 NRSV

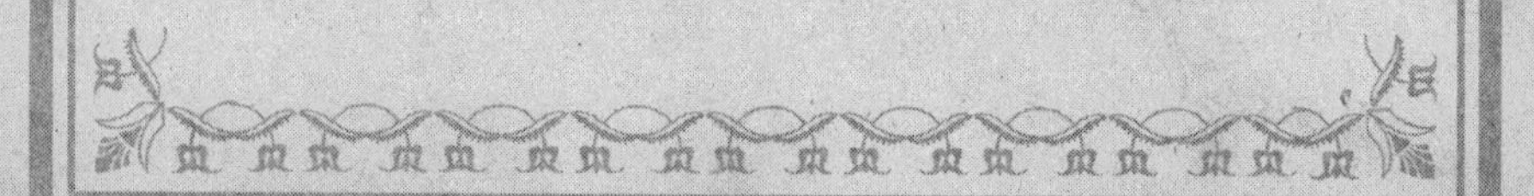

When we grow discouraged, God, direct our eyes toward spiderwebs spun in a corner and remind us that no hope is too small. At first glance, the webs look like fragile, insignificant strands, but in fact they have amazing strength. And consider what those webs do for the spiders. The webs bring the spiders sustenance. Help us twist our own tiny strands of hope into sturdy ropes of commitment when we take the next step toward the tasks you are calling us to. Amen.

Turmoil is the opposite of peace. We can achieve inner peace by acknowledging our turmoil, then shifting our focus toward the healing we desire.

Father, thank you for helping me recognize my sadness. As I come to you for healing, I will keep sight of both the beginning and end of my sorrow. Amen.

The Lord is my shepherd, I shall not want. He makes me lie down in green pastures; he leads me beside still waters; he restores my soul.

—Psalm 23:1–3 NRSV

In the Eyes of an Infant

My 30-minute-old grandson taught me something I had failed to learn in my 50 years.

My daughter Pam's calls were the only sunny moments between the storms of my life. I was divorced. I had no partner to shoulder financial and other stresses, which included major appliances breaking down as if choreographed and a boss whose priorities shifted like the tides—although less predictably.

I worked all day, and every evening I wrote brochures for other companies. Work left no time for little amenities. For instance, there was no time for a long bubble bath with candles or for a pot of homemade soup. God, who once led me beside the still waters and restored my soul, did not seem to be listening to my long overdue need for a green pasture.

Pam lived two states away. I carried the plane schedule and my phone in my purse. My suitcase was in my car.

She called at 3:00 A.M., and I was on a plane before dawn. During the flight, I could not use my cell phone. My dash from plane to taxi allowed no time for dialing. I gave the driver directions and fumbled for the phone. "This is Pam's mom," I said. The doula Pam hired to coach her through labor answered, "No! You're a GRANDMA!"

I was beside myself with joy. The driver drove faster. The sun had just risen, and the hospital seemed to sparkle like a palace.

The birthing room was the greenest pasture of my life. My daughter looked radiant, and my grandson—just 30 minutes old—was in my arms. For two weeks my only work would be to care for these two precious people.

I looked into my grandson's eyes. Pam said, "He knows you love him." My heart overflowed with love for them both. I knew I had to give them more than the example I was setting of working too hard to enjoy life.

My struggles as a single woman were small compared to the struggles Pam faced. She was a single mother. She was responsible, and she was determined. I could see her following my example of working too much and being too tired to enjoy the priceless moments of parenting.

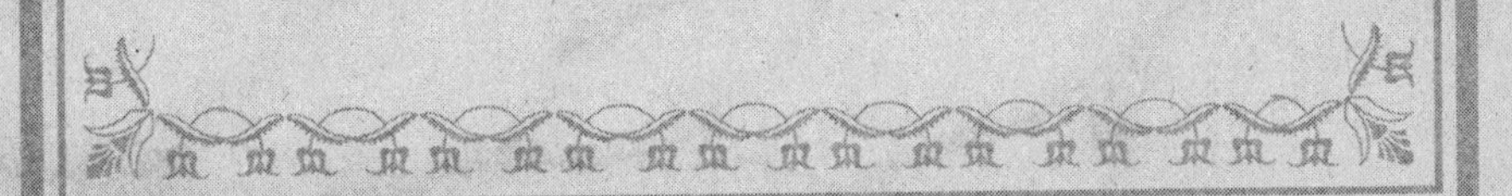

The two weeks I had expected to share with them became six months. Pam's work extended her maternity leave, so she and Max moved in with me. I quit my second job. Through prayer and commitment to my new vow, I learned to live on what I earned at one job.

Pam paid attention to my budget slashing. My rewards were happy evenings and weekends. When Pam moved out, I knew they would be okay. She had her priorities straight—and so did I. But the house seemed too quiet. On the other hand, I had time for that long bubble bath.

Dear God, help us work to live instead of living just to work. Lead us to the green pastures where we can enjoy the companionship of our loved ones and the pleasures that restore us. Amen.

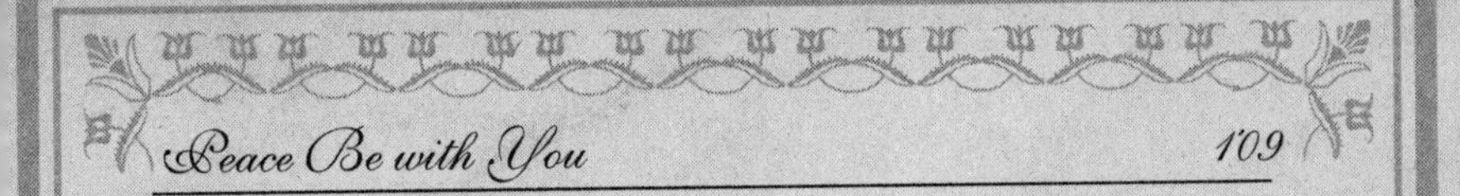

Dear God, I long to feel the peace you bring, the peace that passes all understanding. Fill my entire being with the light of your love, your grace, and your everlasting mercy. Be the soft place that I might fall upon to find the rest and renewal I seek. Amen.

In returning and rest you shall be saved; in quietness and in trust shall be your strength.

—Isaiah 30:15 NRSV

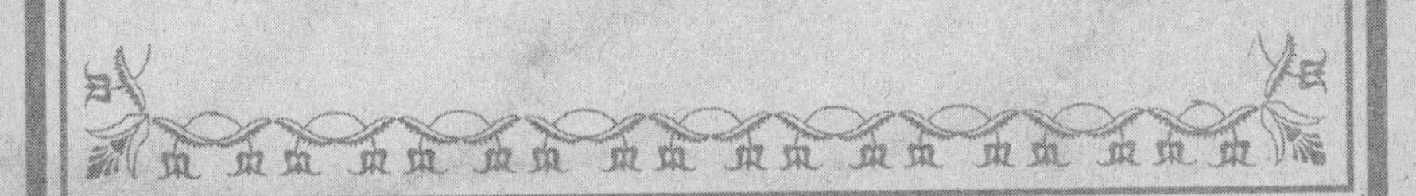

I am the Lord, I have called you in righteousness, I have taken you by the hand and kept you; I have given you as a covenant to the people, a light to the nations.

—Isaiah 42:6 NRSV

When we struggle in unfamiliar territory, Lord, we feel your calming, guiding hand and remember that you have always been faithful to your children. Then we know that our journey is safe. Please continue to give us confidence as we move to where you are calling us.

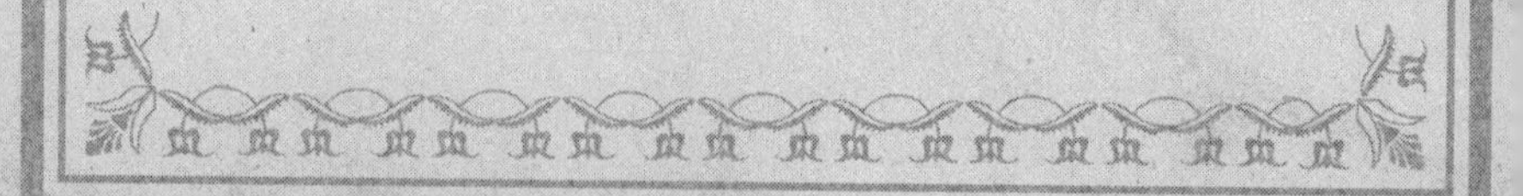

Those who hope in the Lord will renew their strength. They will soar on wings...; they will run and not grow weary, they will walk and not be faint.

—Isaiah 40:31 NIV

Without rhyme or reason, hope allays the soul's worries with the certainty of geese who know precisely the day to fly south.

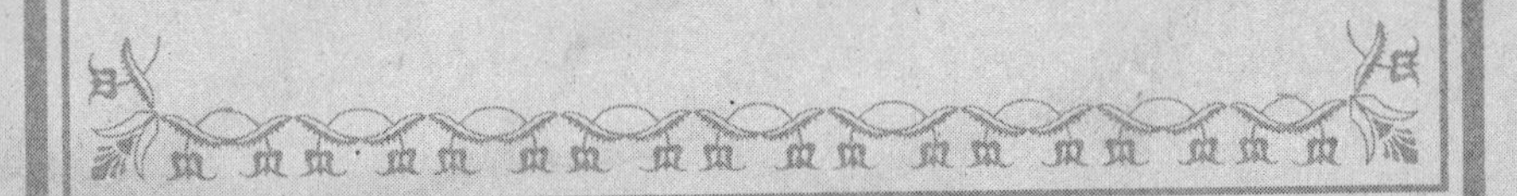

From the Ashes Comes Hope

The Lord is good, a stronghold in a day of trouble; he protects those who take refuge in him.

—Nahum 1:7–8 NRSV

Then they cried to the Lord in their trouble, and he saved them from their distress; he sent out his word and healed them, and delivered them from destruction.

—Psalm 107:19–20 NRSV

Father, hold us in your arms in the midst of devastation and ruin. Remind us that rampaging nature and human evil will not touch us in our eternal homes. Send your angels to remind us that our lives and homes on earth are part of the journey, not our final destination. Amen.

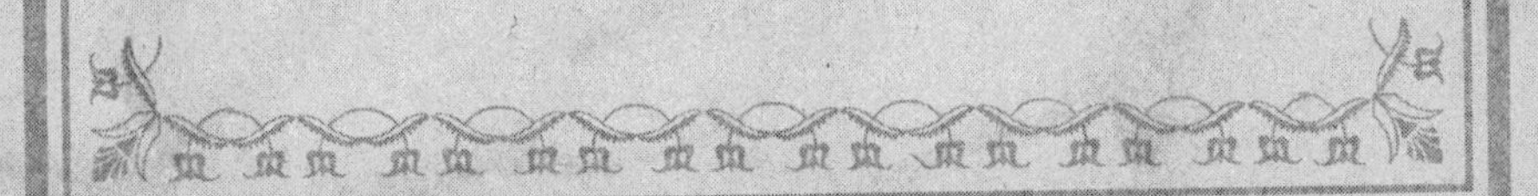

The steadfast love of the Lord never ceases, his mercies never come to an end; they are new every morning; great is your faithfulness.

—LAMENTATIONS 3:22–24 NRSV

Dear Heavenly Father, life is full of surprises. Of course, we welcome the good, but when the bad befalls us, we seek reasons for it. It is often in these bad circumstances that we realize how significant and meaningful our faith is. As a result, we pray that you will teach us to always reach out to you. Amen.

Save me, O God, for the waters have come up to my neck. I sink in deep mire, where there is no foothold; I have come into deep waters, and the flood sweeps over me. I am weary with my crying; my throat is parched. My eyes grow dim with waiting for my God. . . . Answer me, O Lord, for your steadfast love is good.

—Psalm 69:1–3, 16 NRSV

O Lord, I can hardly wait for your answer. Please remind me that love is patient. Amen.

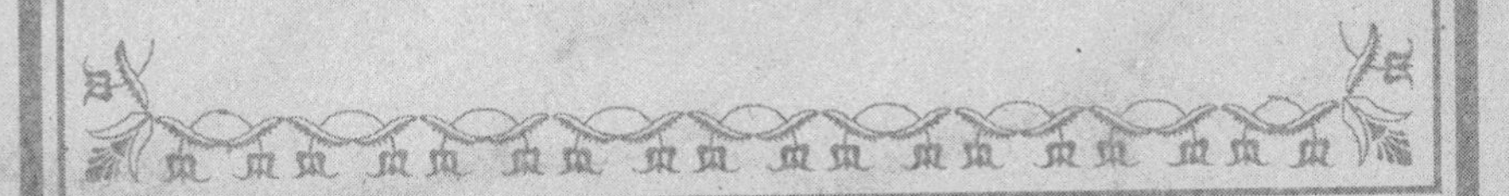

How often we look upon God as our last and feeblest resource! We go to him because we have nowhere else to go. And then we learn that the storms of life have driven us, not upon the rocks, but into the desired haven.

—George MacDonald

Knowing that you are my true home gives me comfort in a world where there are no guarantees and where nothing is permanent. Thank you for being my constant dwelling place. Amen.

When the earth and all its people quake, it is I who hold its pillars firm.

—PSALM 75:3 NIV

Rebuilding a Life

I had lived in Los Angeles for several years working in the entertainment industry and had survived a few sizable earthquakes. Still, nothing could have prepared me for the morning of January 17, 1994, when my whole world came crashing down around me, and my very foundation was rocked to the core.

The Northridge Earthquake occurred around 4:21 A.M., on a cold winter night even for Southern California. This was no ordinary quake. It was violent and brutal, the shaking

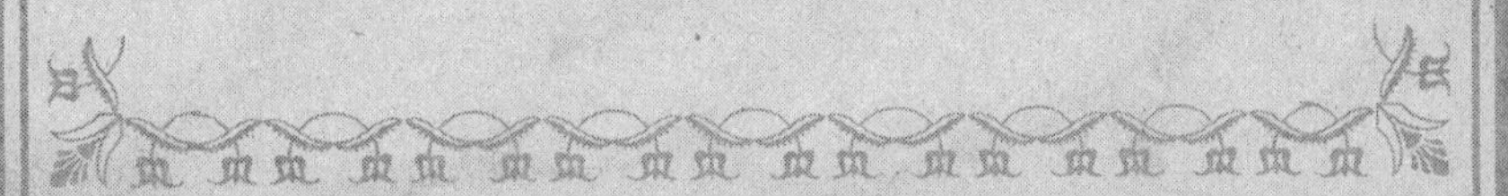

motions so jerky and rough that my husband and I were both thrown off the bed we clung to as furniture and glass flew and smashed to the floor around us. It seemed as though the shaking lasted for over an hour, even though it was only a moment or two, and then the silence that followed was deafening.

We took a quick glance at our two-bedroom apartment: It looked like a war zone. But we had no time to care. We grabbed what we could and ran outside, desperate to get outdoors before the first aftershock.

We stood in the cold for hours with dozens of other terrified victims as the neighborhood around us burned from gas fires. We had little idea until three days later, when our power came back on, what the real damage was.

When a natural disaster occurs, more than just material objects are damaged. Faith is

shaken, and security is destroyed. We wandered around the next few weeks in a state of numb shock trying to pick up the pieces of our apartment, most of which was destroyed beyond repair, as well as our lives. As the aftershocks continued, we lived in a constant state of hypervigilance. Many nights we slept in our car, afraid to be inside. I had loved living in L.A. and pursuing my dreams of being a screenwriter, but now all I wanted was to be safe and secure.

I began to realize that the Northridge Earthquake was a wake-up call that shook the very foundation of my life and my faith in God. My priorities also went through a shake-up, and I found myself looking deeper within for the things that made me happy, safe, and secure.

I longed to be closer to my family in San Diego, as did my husband. Seven months later, we left L.A., uncertain and afraid, but in our hearts we knew it was right. From the rubble of the quake we created a whole new life, closer to those we love. My dreams of writing have taken off in ways I never could have imagined in Los Angeles. It's almost as if God knew I needed the earthquake in order to rearrange my life and rebuild my foundation of faith.

I lost so much during that frightening time, but what I gained was far greater, and for that I am grateful to God.

God, you are my unshakable foundation. You are my unbending column of strength and hope when all seems lost. In the darkest hour, you are the beacon of light that guides me to the safety of solid ground. For all that you are to me, dear God, I am grateful. Amen.

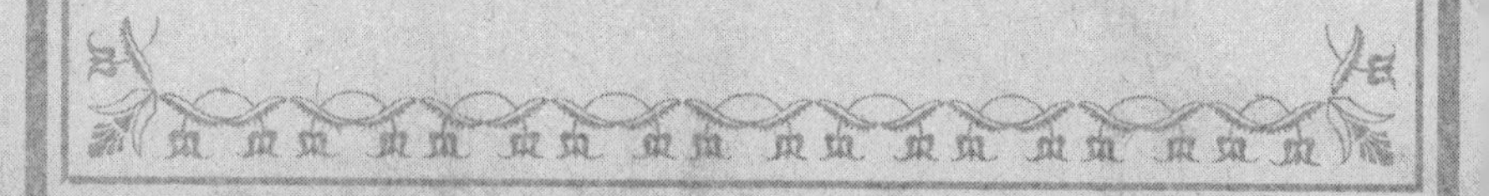

Be strong and courageous; do not be frightened or dismayed, for the Lord your God is with you wherever you go.

—Joshua 1:9 NRSV

In the aftermath of tragedy, it takes energy and courage to rebuild, Great Architect. How amazing that your gift of courage translates worry into energy and fear into determination. Help us recognize ill feelings as potential fuel that can be turned into reconstruction tools. Through your grace, we've courageously faced what was our lives and we are now off to see what our lives can be.

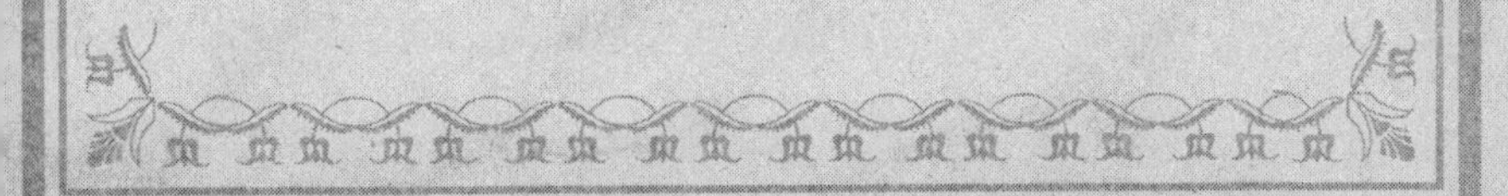

He will cover you with his pinions, and under his wings you will find refuge.
—Psalm 91:4 NRSV

We are grateful, O God, for glimpses we are given of you during times like these. Thank you for showing us how, during raging winds, the mother cardinal refuses to move, standing like a mighty shelter over the fledglings beneath her wings. Secure us in the truth that we, the children of your heart, are likewise watched over and protected during life's storms.

Even if now for a little while you have had to suffer various trials, so that the genuineness of your faith—being more precious than gold that, though perishable, is tested by fire—may be found to result in praise and glory and honor.

—1 PETER 1:6–7 NRSV

Reborn of Fire

The flames licked at the sides of the hills just above my home. I stood there, enrapt and frozen with fear at the wall of fire that mercilessly descended the dry landscape.

I had little time to pack up anything when the evacuation order came down for my small

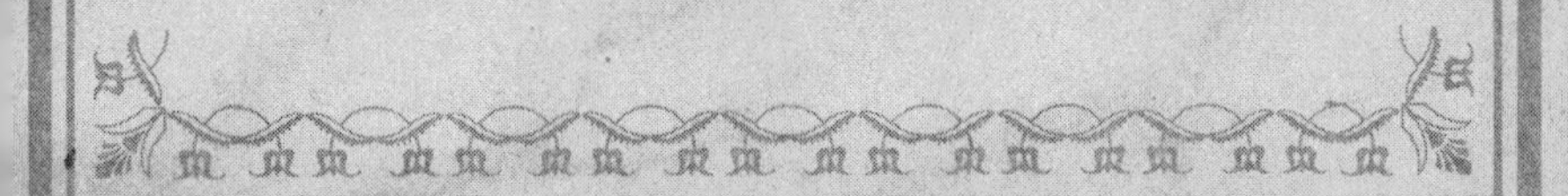

rural town. The raging brushfire had started in an easterly direction, but strong Colorado winds had kicked in and turned the fire on its heels. Now it was only yards away from the perimeter of my four-acre property.

I quickly grabbed a few valuables and piled into my car. As I sped away, I realized I had left behind so many things and wished I could have had just five more minutes to think more clearly. I glanced in my rear-view mirror with the thought of going back, but the wall of fire was unmistakably close.

I stayed with my brother, Will, who lived about 15 miles away. We watched the local news coverage of the fire, and at one point I actually saw my house in the background, engulfed in flames.

After the fire was out and the firefighters said it was okay, Will went with me to survey the

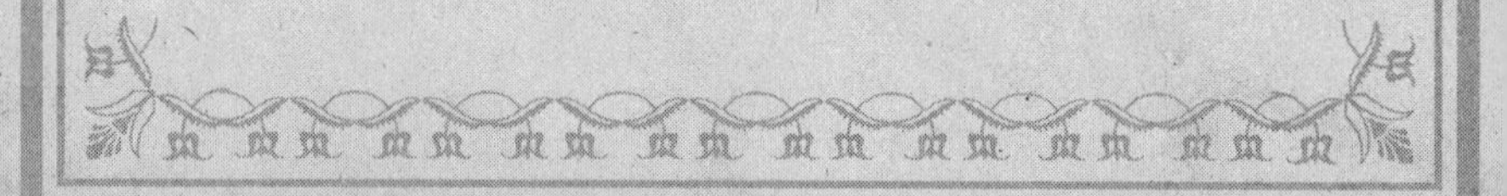

damage. We walked silently, looking for anything that might have survived the blaze. I was angry with God as I looked down at what was once my grandmother's jewelry box, a possession I treasured.

You have to lose everything to truly understand the pain and suffering that I was going through. I felt almost ashamed that I hurt so badly. After all, I was okay. But I wept for my home the way I would a friend gone forever.

That evening back at Will's, I drank tea alone on Will's porch. I felt small below the sea of stars and planets. A breeze moved my hair against my shoulder, ever so softly. I suddenly felt so expansive, so a part of everything around me, including the fire that continued to burn to the west.

I closed my eyes and let the feeling of unity wash over me. God had not let me down. It was

a fire and only a fire. I had made the choice to live in the back country, where fires occurred all the time. God had given me free will, and now I also had the free will to accept my loss and move on.

The next day, I went back to the fire site and saw not my old home but a new opportunity for growth, renewal, and rebirth. I thanked God as I walked away, sad but eager to begin again.

Blessed Creator, I long to feel a sense of unity and harmony with all that you have created. Help me to understand that natural disasters are opportunities for renewal and that around every storm cloud, a silver lining waits for the one who has faith in you. Let it be.

This present tragedy is so overwhelming, O God. Please give me eyes of faith to see change and healing. Amen.

Faith offers a new way of life, where everything can be used for good.

For everything created by God is good, and nothing is to be rejected.

—1 Timothy 4:4 NRSV

Be merciful unto me, O God, be merciful unto me: for my soul trusteth in thee: yea, in the shadow of thy wings will I make my refuge, until these calamities be overpast.

—PSALM 57:1 KJV

When the storms of life surround us, Lord, we cannot see the light of the sun behind the clouds, and so we forget it is there. The winds blow hard upon us, and the cold air chills us, but once the storm has passed, we stand in the sun again, and we find we have been cleansed.

The Lord is my rock, my fortress, and my deliverer.

—Psalm 18:2 NRSV

God, how much longer must I stay curled up in a ball behind this large stone, seeking protection from the storm that swirls around me? I have watched the weeds bow and bend and still not break against the onslaught of the wind. God, I sense I must bend and bow in the midst of the strong forces that pummel me. Then I will find strength to endure until the morning light comes, when I will stand once again because of your help.

And we know that all things work together for good to them that love God, to them who are called according to His purpose.

—ROMANS 8:28 KJV

Flooded

I watched on TV as people were forced from their homes, flooded out, all their belongings left behind. Rising rivers pushed over their banks, overwhelming volunteers fighting to save homes, stores, schools, and churches. But nothing could resist the churning waters.

I saw dirty, tired, defeated faces pass by. Some had spent days fighting the flood. Some hadn't slept at all. Some hadn't bothered to eat,

more concerned with saving their towns if they possibly could.

But the rising waters washed away everything in their paths. Some people had time to cram what they could in cars. But many more left with what few clothes they were wearing and an armload of belongings. They were forced to give up and flee for their very lives.

I continued to watch, feeling more and more ashamed of myself. The worst I'd ever faced was my so-called "flooded" basement: an inch or two of water coming in half a dozen times over the years. I'd never experienced the sort of tragedy facing these people losing their homes only a few hours away from where I lived, high and safely dry.

Watching the weary, disheartened faces, I wished I were rich and could replace everything for all of them. Then I heard of a group provid-

ing a truck. Anyone in my area who wanted to help could bring donations for the flood victims to the truck. This was something I could do.

Eagerly, I searched my own comfortable home for whatever we could spare, such as linens, clothes, toys, and canned food. My whole family helped, gathering items we hardly used or could do without. The kids donated some of their toys for children who had nothing left.

When I got to the parking lot where the truck sat waiting, I was stunned. Tables stood stacked high with canned food, sorted into categories. Great heaps of clothing lay spread on tables to be sifted through and boxed up. Toys piled up in another spot, some still in packaging. Baby supplies filled bag after bag.

Cars and more cars entered the lot, bringing donations, until one volunteer joked to the crowd, "I think we'll need a bigger truck!"

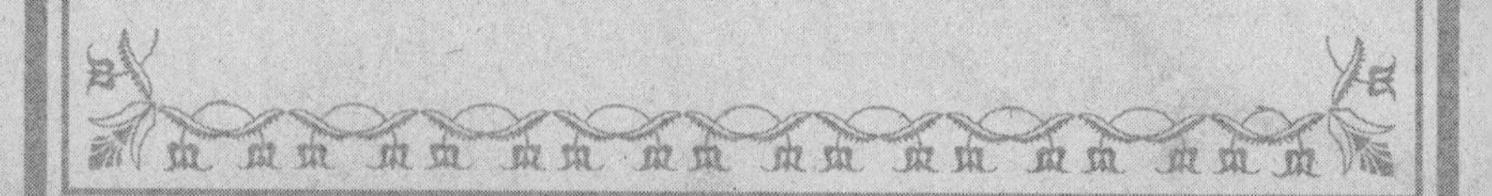

Everyone laughed at his joke. It felt good to laugh as we worked to help others. But it was true. They did need a bigger truck. They needed several bigger trucks by the time our city had finished pouring out donations.

Even as I laughed with the crowd, I felt hot tears on my cheeks. And, looking out at the vast sea of food and clothing, I thought this new flood would help and heal. God had touched hundreds of hearts, so that a flood of caring, compassion, and love filled those trucks to overflowing.

Almighty God, sometimes the floods of life leave us devastated and defeated. Our tears flow like rivers pushing over their banks. In our worst moments, you give us comfort and hope. Amen.

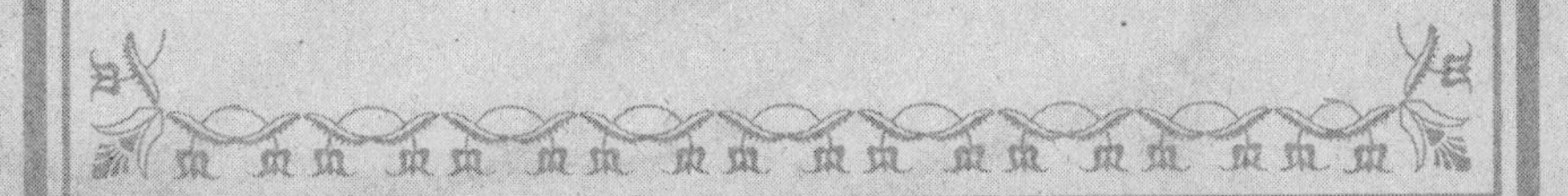

The wind blows where it chooses, and you hear the sound of it, but you do not know where it comes from or where it goes. So it is with everyone who is born of the Spirit.

—John 3:8 NRSV

When the winds of change and challenge blow hard into my life, I will take refuge in you, O Lord. Although I cannot see you, I know you are always with me, O Lord, and in that I take comfort and find strength.

I am sorrowful after this great tragedy. It feels like this is more than I can bear. Yet I know just crying with others is one way to share the burden. Thank you for other survivors and thank you for healing tears, Father. May they flow freely and turn quickly into the joy that you promise will come.

Those who sow in tears will reap with songs of joy.

—Psalm 126:5 NIV

You who have made me see many troubles and calamities will revive me again; from the depths of the earth you will bring me up again. You will . . . comfort me once again.

—Psalm 71:20–21 NRSV

Thank you, God, for letting me survive this tragedy. I am glad that I have been given another chance in this world. Although it will be hard to start over, I realize that this is an opportunity for me to decide the importance of things. Please comfort me as I consider this. Amen.

I am not sure how to go on. I am completely devastated. My possessions and my home are now nothing more than dust. Please remind me that you, Creator, formed humans from dust. Console me with the knowledge that I can create beauty from these ruins. Amen.

When the quiet after the storm finally comes to our hearts, we look up to find that God is still with us, holding us close to his heart.

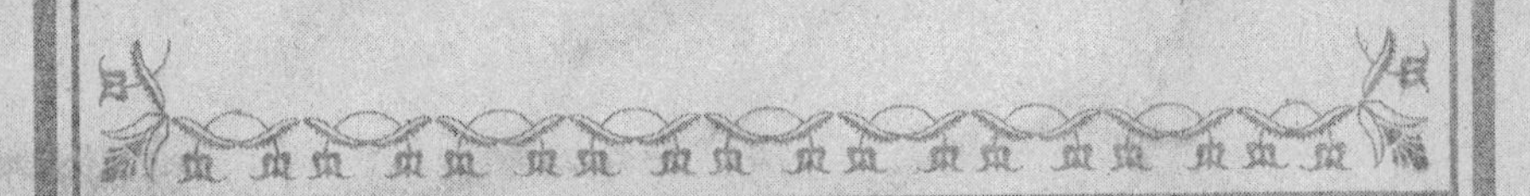

You're Not Alone

*T*he Lord is near to all who call on him.

—Psalm 145:18 NRSV

God, you are invisible but not unseen. You reveal yourself in creation and demonstrate your kindness in a stranger's sincere smile. You are intangible but not unfelt. You caress our faces with the wind and embrace us in a friend's arms. We look for you and feel your presence. Amen.

O taste and see that the Lord is good; happy are those who take refuge in him.

—Psalm 34:8 NRSV

I will seek the lost, and I will bring back the strayed, and I will bind up the injured, and I will strengthen the weak.

—EZEKIEL 34:16 NRSV

Grace of my heart, I turn to you when I am feeling lost and alone. You restore me with strength and hope and the courage to face a new day. You bless me with joy and comfort me through trials and tribulations. You direct my thoughts, guide my actions, and temper my words. You give me the patience and kindness I need to be good. Grace of my heart, I turn to you. Amen.

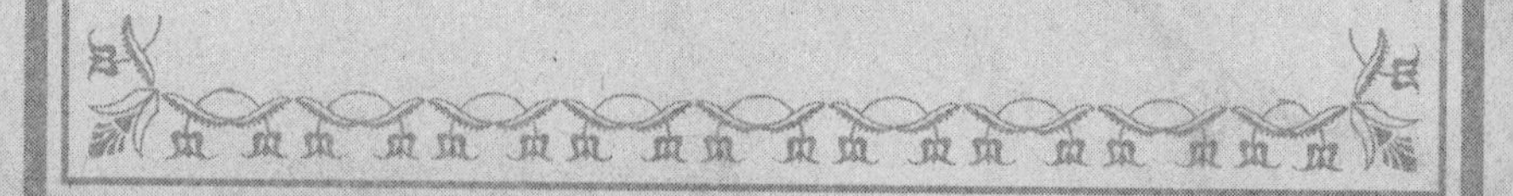

*D*raw near to God, and he will draw near to you.

—JAMES 4:8 NRSV

Woman at the Well

*A*fter my uncle died, I moved to England. I did not see my Aunt Ruth until my vacation a year later. Our good-bye visit before I moved had saddened me despite my excitement over being transferred to the London office. Ruth had given up her friends and music to make a vocation of her sorrow. She was living alone, and her home was a shrine to her dead husband. She took little interest in herself. Her conversation was limited to "Ben planted that tree. . . . Ben gave me this vase. . . . Ben always said. . . ."

A year later, when I walked into her house and hugged her, I knew that the season of her bitter sorrow had passed. Sheet music was scattered on the piano, and a beaded wall hanging had replaced her Monet print.

Over lunch, my adventures in London were just as exciting as her adventures in Louisville. Aunt Ruth was a retired teacher, and she was using her skills to teach English to women from India, Thailand, and China as well as all over Europe. Her friend from India—who had given her that wall hanging—invited her to Bombay.

"You've never even been out of the country, and you're going to Bombay!" I exclaimed.

"Yes, my passport photo makes me look like an inmate," she said. "Ben would insist I have a new photo taken. Oh, I miss him!"

"But you aren't the woman I left a year ago," I said.

She put down her teacup. "It's not something that could be put in a letter." Her smile was radiant, and her story is my greatest legacy:

"One night after I had pleaded with God to call me home, I picked up my Bible. I read about the woman at the well. She gave Jesus a cup of water. He took it and said, 'I will give you the living water.' I prayed that Jesus would give me the living water.

"The next morning as I was crying and dusting Ben's pictures on the piano, I remembered how proud Ben was of my music. I dried my tears and started playing. It had been so long that I was like a child, a little afraid but fascinated by finger exercises. I was playing more for Ben than for me. Gradually my music came back, and it was no longer enough to play for Ben. I started playing the organ at church again. Then a note in the church bulletin caught my

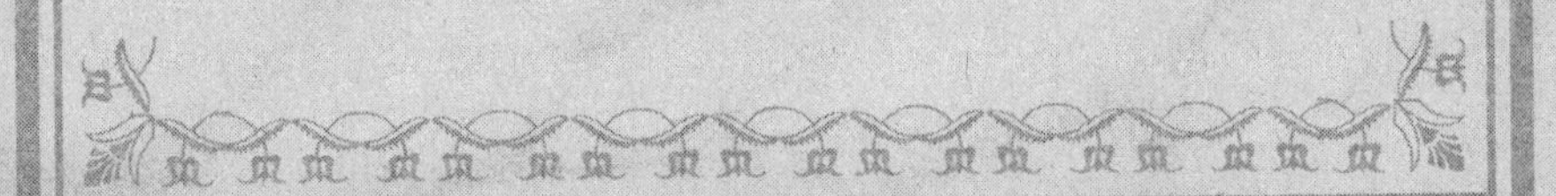

eye. They had a program to help foreign women adjust to our culture. ”

“But India!” I said. “I was going to invite you to England.”

“After India, I’m going to China to visit another lady I taught,” she said. “I’m saving England for when I’m older.”

Ten years later, we went to England. She had traveled all over the world. She did not look a day older than her passport photo. The living water still flowed through her spirit. Everyone we met seemed touched by it and wanted to linger a bit longer in her presence.

Father, your grace can refresh and renew us with the living water of hope and faith. Please help us fully live the lives you have given us. Amen.

I can do all things through him who strengthens me.

—PHILLIPPIANS 4:13 NRSV

As we learn to trust you, God, we discover your strengthening presence in various places and people. Wherever we encounter shelter, comfort, rest, and peace, we are bound to hear your voice, welcoming us. And in whomever we find truth, love, gentleness, and humility, we are sure to hear your heartbeat, assuring us that you will always be near. Thank you, God. Amen.

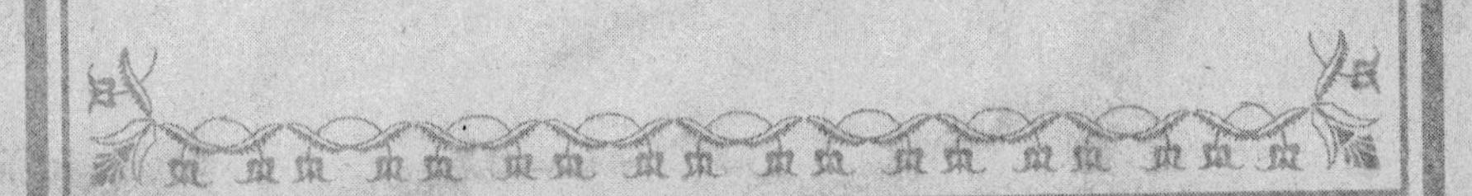

O Lord, we give thanks for your presence, which greets us each day in the guise of a friend, a work of nature, or a story from a stranger. We are reminded through these messengers in our times of deepest need that you are indeed watching over us. Lord, we have known you in the love and care of a friend, who envelopes and keeps us company in our despair. When we observe the last morning glory stretching faithfully to receive what warmth is left in the chilly sunshine, we are heartened and inspired to do the same. When we are hesitant to speak up and then read in the newspaper a story of courage and controversy, we find our voice lifted and strengthened by your message in black-and-white type. Lord, we are grateful receivers of all the angelic messages that surround us every day.

You who live in the shelter of the Most High, who abide in the shadow of the Almighty, will say to the Lord, "My refuge and my fortress; my God, in whom I trust."

—PSALM 9:1–2 NRSV

Our Father, remind us that to live a life of faith is to live always in your presence, at peace in the home of your love. Amen.

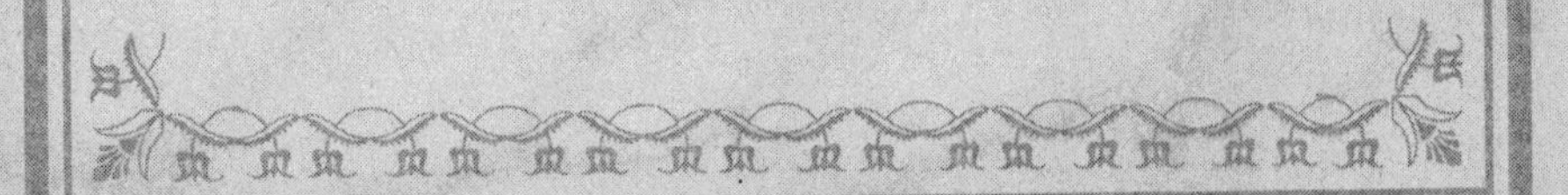

*W*hen we seek God, we find ourselves,
for God is right here within us.

The Crossing

I stood at the corner of Johnson and University streets as cars and trucks whizzed by at breakneck speeds. Horns were blaring, tires were screeching, and people were yelling at one another. The sound of the noon-hour traffic echoed in my ears. My faithful guide dog, Miss Ginny, was at the vet's office for the day, and I was alone, trying to cross the busy metropolitan street. My hands were trembling, and a million butterflies danced the two-step in my stomach.

I should have stayed home. I shouldn't have tried to do this alone. I should have taken the day off of

work. I should have called a taxi. All these thoughts raced through my mind. I was frightened, but I had come this far, and it was too late to turn back now.

I felt along the sidewalk with the tip of my cane until I found the edge of the curb. I was terrified to step off into the busy intersection, but I was running late for work and had to hurry.

"Excuse me, please. Are you crossing this street?" I heard a young man's voice as he walked up beside me.

"I'm trying to," I said. "The traffic is so heavy today, and people are driving like there's no tomorrow."

"I know," he replied. "I hate crossing Johnson Street, especially at lunchtime. This is a scary intersection, isn't it?"

I answered, "Yes."

"May I take your arm, and we can cross together?"

The young man reached out and grasped my arm. His grip was firm on my elbow as we stepped together into the rushing traffic. I felt my way on the arm of this kind young stranger. As we crossed the street together, I said a quick prayer of thanks that this gentleman had offered to help me.

I heard the traffic pattern change just as the toe of my right foot touched the curb on the far side of Johnson Street. With the young man's assistance, I had made it across the street unharmed. I sighed in relief and patted his hand gratefully.

"Ma'am, you will never know how much I appreciate you helping me across the street. This intersection always frightens me. I feel lucky to have had you here."

"Helping *you* across the street?" His statement puzzled me.

"Yes, ma'am," he replied. "It isn't easy for a blind man to negotiate such a busy intersection, and this crossing is always particularly frightening for me."

I was completely taken aback. *Oh my stars! I just crossed six lanes of very busy traffic on the arm of someone who's as blind as I am!*

My lips quivered as I spoke. "Are you okay? I didn't realize you were blind."

The young man laughed. "Of course I'm okay. Aren't you? And as for being blind, I thought that was pretty obvious. Didn't you see my cane?"

"Your blindness was not obvious to me, and no. . . I didn't see your cane. I didn't notice it at all." My speech was broken, and my voice trembled.

The young man laughed. "Thanks again. I'm pretty lucky. Whenever I need a helping hand, someone always shows up just in time. Have a nice day."

My hands stopped shaking, and a sudden calmness came over me, a calmness I hadn't experienced in a long time. "Sir, I hope you have a good day, too, and don't be afraid of this street crossing. I think you're right. Whenever we are most afraid, someone comes along to help us. Sometimes they even help us find courage we didn't know we had. Thank you for letting me help you. You helped me, too."

You are safe in the care of the Lord your God.

—1 Samuel 25:29 TLB

Calm me enough, O Lord, to breathe deeply and restoratively. Prayer restores me in the presence of all that threatens to undo me, which I name to you now.

Just as a frantic dog trapped in a drain pipe crawls to safety toward the sound of its master's voice, so too can all of us feeling so lost and frightened move toward the voice of love.

Lord God, you will never leave us or forsake us. You are always near, always watching over us. We will never be alone as long as you are here with us. We do not need to worry or be anxious. We can trust in you. Amen and amen.

It is you who light my lamp; the Lord, my God, lights up my darkness.

—Psalm 18:28 NRSV

I would rather walk with God in the dark than go alone in the light.

—Mary Gardiner Brainard, *Not Knowing*

Dear God, thank you for being my light. Amen.

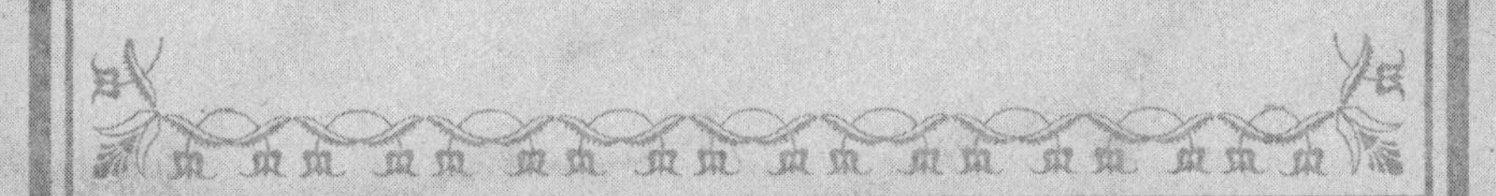

In my distress I cried unto the Lord,
and he heard me.

—Psalm 120:1 KJV

While I wait for this piercing pain of loneliness to pass, Great Comforter, cradle me as the wailing, lost child I've become. Closing my eyes and breathing deeply, I feel your warming presence as a blanket tossed around my shoulders and know that no matter how lost I feel right now, you hold the most important truth, whispering it now: "You are my beloved child. I am with you."

How comforting, Steadfast God, to know that you tend us as we move through life's extremes. You are there with us in births and deaths, in stillness and activity. We find the courage to live through these present moments and to move into the future, knowing that we cannot wander so far in any direction that you are not already there.

God's loving knowledge of each of his children forms an unbreakable parenthesis within which to rest, heal, and recover.

But when in their distress they turned to the Lord, the God of Israel, and sought him, he was found by them.

—2 CHRONICLES 15:4 NRSV

No matter the worries I have, small or large, you, O God, are there ahead of me with promises of help and support that relieve me and free me from getting stuck in the mire of my fears. I am grateful.

Casting out Fear

Sheri decided to take the side streets because the traffic report warned that the freeway was backed up for miles. She needed to get home to see her son off to bed and to let the baby-sitter go home. Her husband was on a business trip and would not be home until morning.

She pulled off the freeway, maneuvered the one-way streets, and turned onto one she was certain connected with Main Street. She ended up in a totally unfamiliar area. She backtracked and turned onto another unfamiliar street.

The neighborhood seemed seedy. A group of young men hung out on the corner, watching her as she drove by. She stared straight ahead, terrified to make eye contact.

Sheri found herself on a dark stretch of industrial area. Not another soul was in sight. She felt panic rising, but she was determined to get herself back to the main road, where she would just get back on the freeway.

That's when she heard the thudding noise. The car lurched to the right. Sheri knew the sound and the feel of a flat tire. She stopped on the shoulder and took out her cell phone, but she could not get a signal. *Great,* she thought, *alone in a bad neighborhood with a flat tire and no cell phone signal. It couldn't get much worse.*

But it did. Sheri heard a noise behind the car, and she saw in the rearview mirror a group of young thugs approaching the car. Sheri recognized them as the gang on the street corner. As they came closer, her blood froze in her veins. She dared not breathe. She began to pray for help, begging God to come to her aid and pro-

tect her. All she wanted to do was to get home to her baby and to hold him close.

She closed her eyes, praying out loud now. Over and over she repeated the words *Perfect love casts out fear.* It gave her relief, until one of the gang members knocked on her window. He was smiling. Sheri kept praying silently as he asked if she needed help. She could barely nod her head yes, she was so petrified.

The kid motioned for her to get out, and Sheri's life flashed before her eyes. Afraid they might be armed, Sheri got out.

She saw two of them with a tire jack, and her heart caught in her throat. One of them asked for the trunk key. She handed it over silently, still uncertain of her fate. The kid opened the trunk and removed her spare tire. He jacked up her car, then deftly he took off the old tire and replaced it.

The kid grinned at Sheri. That's when she realized God had come to her aid. In fact, one of the kids even told her directions to the freeway.

As Sheri pulled away, they waved good-bye to her. She found the freeway, and when she got home, her son was fast asleep. She sat beside him, just loving him and feeling a sense of overwhelming gratitude. God had protected her. She had truly not been alone, even in her darkest hour. In fact, Sheri was quite certain those boys had been messengers of God.

God of All Comfort, I know that with you by my side I am never alone. Your perfect love casts out all fear, doubt, and uncertainty. Your presence emboldens and empowers me. You are the light that leads me to safety again. Amen.

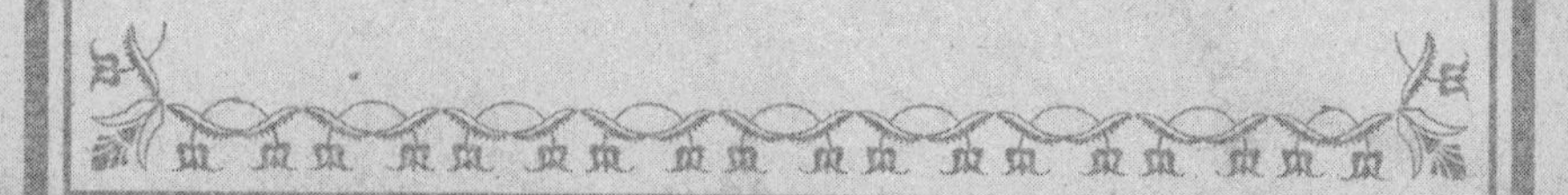

God is everything to us and his creation. He is our breath and our life. He is that which makes the sun to rise and the birds to sing. When we call out to God and open ourselves to him, we invite life itself to perch on our shoulder.

Father God, as we journey through life, remind us of your presence. Let us see your love in everything. Amen.

Unless the Lord builds the house,
those who build it labor in vain.

—Psalm 127:1 NRSV

You are the foundation of my life. When circumstances shift and make my world unsteady, you remain firm. When threats of what lies ahead blow against the framework of my thoughts, you are solid. When I focus on your steadfastness, I realize that you are my strength for the moment, the one sure thing in my life. Because of you I stand now, and I will stand tomorrow as well because you are there already. Amen.

Let all who take refuge in you rejoice; let them ever sing for joy. Spread your protection over them, so that those who love your name may exult in you.

—Psalm 5:11 NRSV

If I did not believe in you, God, the depth of my loneliness and despair would be inconsolable. But I know you are real, for you have always consoled me. Please comfort and console the most vulnerable, hurting places in my heart this day. Please be with me. Amen.

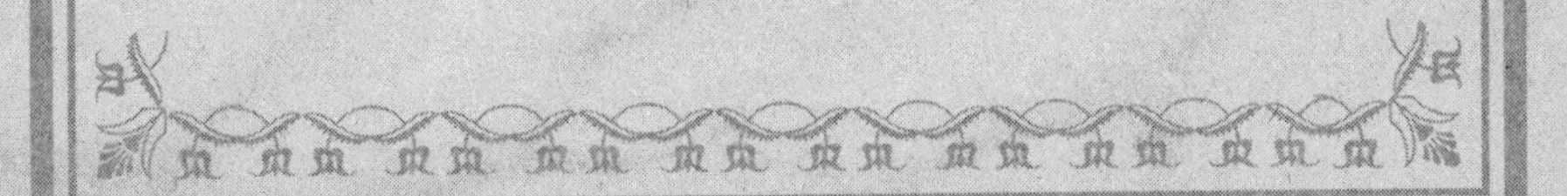

Heavenly Comfort

Blessed are those who mourn, for they will be comforted.
—Matthew 5:4 NRSV

The Lord gave, and the Lord has taken away; blessed be the name of the Lord.

—Job 1:21 NRSV

O Lord in heaven, I am hurting. My whole world seems to have collapsed around me, and I fear the emptiness in my soul will consume me. Help me in my grief, Lord. Day by day, lift a bit of the heaviness from my heart. Moment by moment, fill me with your comfort. Assure me that by your grace there is hope even though today is filled with pain and loss. Thank you, Lord. Amen.

To every thing there is a season, and a time to every purpose under the heaven.

—Ecclesiastes 3:1 KJV

A Final Blessing

When my beloved grandfather died, I was not at his funeral. I had chosen instead to visit him while he was still alive, struggling with the final stages of colon cancer. I knew that I could only travel once from my home with my limited budget and job schedule, and I chose instead to spend two weeks with a man I loved while he could still see and hear me.

When I arrived in San Diego, I was shocked to see how haggard my grandmother had

become. She had been spending every moment by her husband's side, and her love for him was heartbreaking. I could feel the tension in her small frame as she hugged me at the airport, and her breath came quick and shallow. The man that she had loved since childhood was dying, and the pain emanated from her tired eyes. She took me to the house, and I ran to my grandfather's bedside. I was shocked. He had always been so robust and healthy, and now he was wasting away from the disease that ravaged him. I spent the next two weeks sitting beside him, watching baseball games, reading to him, or just talking.

On the day I was to leave, he was still hanging on to life. I kissed him good-bye and told him how much I loved him and how dear he was to me. He said I would always be his favorite grandchild, and I reminded him I was his only

grandchild. We laughed. It was an old joke, but we loved it.

Three days later, I got a telephone call from my grandmother. Her voice cracked as she told me my grandfather had gone into a coma soon after I left and died without pain. She asked if I could come back for the funeral, but I explained to her I could not and that it had been more important to me to see him when he was alive. In her pain and despair, my grandmother snapped at me, insinuating I lacked respect for the dead, and she hung up on me. Her words stung, but I knew they came from a place of deep suffering.

The day of the funeral, I remembered my grandfather in my own special way. I could feel his presence and knew he was not angry with me. Still, I hated any bad feelings between my grandmother and myself. I asked God to help

her see my point of view and then released the problem to his loving power and grace.

Three weeks later, my grandmother wrote me a long letter, asking me to forgive her. She told me that she knew that my grandfather had hung on to life just to see me and that when I had left, he told her that my visit was a final blessing to a perfectly wonderful life.

I called my grandmother that evening, and before she could say a word, I told her I loved her dearly. We then talked and laughed about a man we both loved—and missed—dearly.

Dear God, help me do the right thing and follow the dictates of my spirit. Even amidst the harsh judgments of others, show me the path that leads to joy, to truth, and to love. Amen.

Heavenly Father, thank you for the precious gift of memories. May our grief in the passing of those we love be soothed by the years we shared and the ways they touched our lives. May our tears be shed in love.

Every saint in heaven is as a flower in the garden of God, and every soul there is as a note in some concert of delightful music.

—Jonathan Edwards

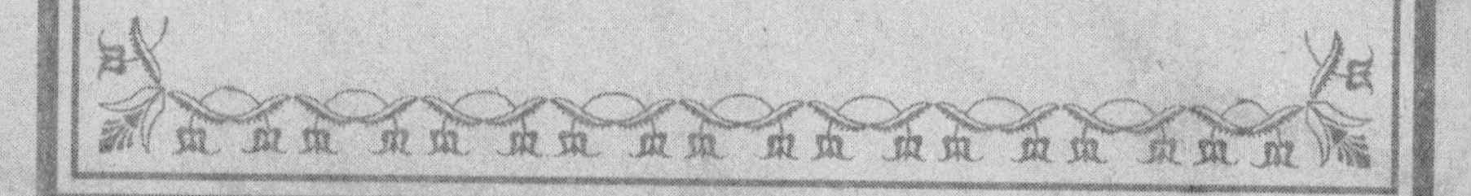

Dear Lord, thank you for reaching out with your hands to catch us when we fall, to hold us safely in your care, and to keep us from harm. Thank you for reminding us that death is not the end—it is the beginning of new life with you. Amen and amen.

Surely goodness and mercy will follow me all the days of my life, and I will dwell in the house of the Lord forever.

—Psalm 23:6 NIV

For this perishable body must put on imperishability, and this mortal body must put on immortality.

—1 Corinthians 15:53 NRSV

We forget sometimes that resurrection is new life, God. Remind us that resurrection is our promise from you and our hope for the future. Please help us believe there is an eternity for which you are preparing us.

God, please hasten the healing. Enter into our broken hearts. Bring mercy, compassion, and wholeness. Let us find strength and determination to rebuild our lives. Amen.

When someone we love dies, God hides a smile in every memory and hope in every tear.

Let go, and let God help. Only by surrendering our weakness over to a higher power can we find the inner strength we need.

I Am with You Always

When Dorothy's husband and best friend of 50 years, Jay, passed away, Dorothy thought her entire world had come to an end. For five decades, they had been inseparable companions and lovers, adventurers going through life together hand in hand and heart to heart. His death came quickly—as he had just the year before been given a clean bill of health—which made Dorothy even less prepared for the emptiness, the denial, and the anger.

Mainly, she was angry at God for taking from her the one person she most loved. She and Jay never had children, simply because they were so in love with their own life together. They had traveled all over the world and done everything they had ever desired. Now that he was gone, Dorothy felt betrayed and confused. She had always been a devout and religious person, but now she felt very little trust in a God that would do something so cruel.

Dorothy had convinced herself that there was no life ahead of her, at least not without Jay. She sank into a deep depression and rarely ventured outside into a world she simply could not bear to encounter without Jay.

On one particularly bad day, when Dorothy actually hoped she would die soon so she could be with Jay, she began to cry and could not stop. The tears blinded and stung her eyes as her

body shook with sobs. It was as if her body was trying to purge all the fear, anger, and loneliness she had felt from the day she buried Jay.

Dorothy lay down on her bed and begged God to free her from her pain. She buried her face into a pillow as a deep wail of agony rose within her. The force of her feelings terrified her, but she could not stop. She had to let them out. All the while she asked God over and over again to help her, to heal her, and to bring her some semblance of peace.

As she lay there, Dorothy felt a warm rush spread through her body as her muscles relaxed and the power of her emotions subsided. She sat up, feeling somehow more focused and clear than she had in a very long time. A smile, barely there at first, formed at the corners of her mouth. For the first time since Jay's passing, she felt a sense of acceptance and of peace. Dorothy

felt a sense of assurance that she was not alone and that God had not let her down after all.

Dorothy realized that once she was freed from the blinding pain, her eyes were now open to see the heavenly comfort of God's love for her, and that Jay was never as far away as the beating of her own heart. It was the beginning of a long road to healing, but Dorothy wasn't afraid, for this was one adventure she would not be taking alone.

Heavenly Father, in the midst of my pain and suffering, be my comfort and peace. In the midst of my fear and loneliness, be my constant companion through the long, dark night. Assure me that I am never alone and that your love for me is enduring, unending, and infinite. Amen.

Many who have lived through the loss of a loved one experience a deeper awareness of everything around them. Life becomes clear and sharp in definition, as if being suddenly seen through perfect eyesight, where before life was blurred and dulled. Perhaps death serves to awaken the living. Perhaps this is death's great blessing.

You have turned my mourning into dancing; you have... clothed me with joy.

—Psalm 30:11 NRSV

Help us live with mystery, O God, for within each question is the possibility of growth, wisdom, and a deeper faith. For with you, we find courage to ask the questions, trusting that some time, maybe without even noticing it, we will discover the answers. Amen.

For now we see in a mirror, dimly; but then we will see face to face. Now I know only in part; then I will know fully, even as I have been fully known.

—1 Corinthians 13:12 NRSV

When the Spirit of truth comes, he will guide you into all truth.

—JOHN 16:13 NRSV

Heavenly Father, help us to know that, to receive truth, we must be willing to face reality. We must not rebel, and this takes courage. We look to you for guidance as we begin this arduous task of changing our thoughts, attitudes, and actions. Walk with us as we accept the truth. Amen.

Yea, though I walk through the valley of the shadow of death, I will fear no evil; for thou art with me.

—Psalm 23:4 KJV

This loss is painful, Lord. Please help me deal with the sad feelings in tangible ways, so the sorrow is alleviated little by little. Please make your presence known to me in this time of need.

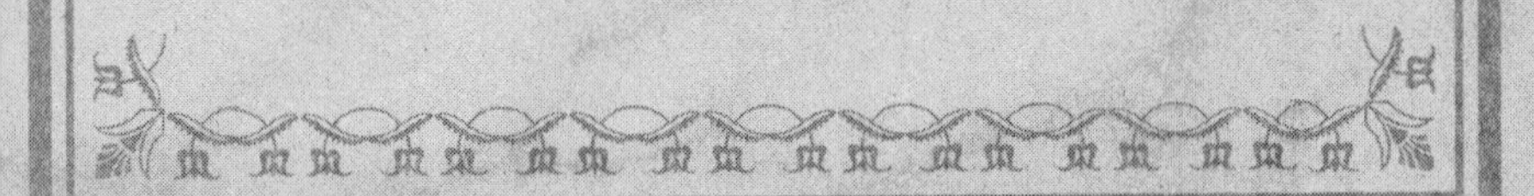

There is a sanctuary that we can retreat to for the comfort and peace we need in times of mourning. This sanctuary is within us, and its doors are always open.

Lord God, let me learn to find the courage to turn away from the heartbreaking loss of the past and look with an open heart toward the possibilities of the future. Let not my own heart die, nor let my capacity to love diminish in the throes of my present anguish. Let me learn to love again. Amen.

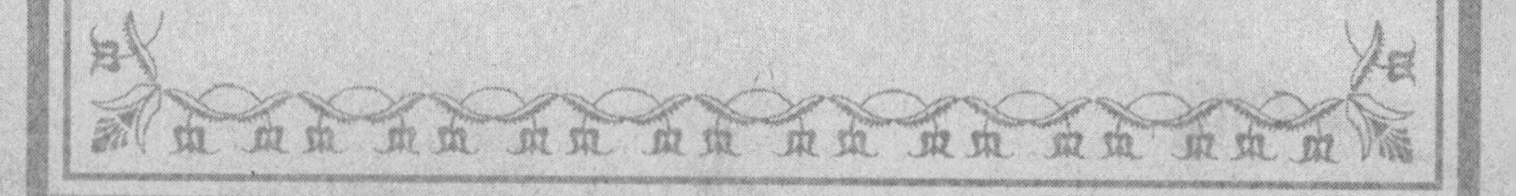

My First Mother's Day Without a Mother

It was Mother's Day, my first without a mother. I had sadly missed selecting a card for and giving a gift to her. I always gave her a book, the one I had enjoyed the most that year. It was the most appropriate gift for the woman who had introduced me to *Little Women, The Canterbury Tales,* and Emily Dickinson's poetry. The book I would have sent her this year sat on my bookshelf.

I was dressed for church, standing in my living room, and surveying the mess of crumpled newspapers, empty juice glasses, and used tissues. My husband and children were suffering with an unrelentless cold that I had managed to escape so far. Last year they had served me breakfast and we had called my mother. This morning I had served them oatmeal, but no one could eat. When I got home from church, I would heat up chicken soup.

I kissed them good-bye and walked to church feeling lonely and sad. A Sunday school teacher greeted me at the door. She was standing beside a tray of corsages: violets, pansies, and lilies of the valley. I had heard rumors of this project from my children. What surprised me was the little spray of lilies the teacher selected for me. "I know your mother passed away," she said softly. "Wear this for her." She pinned the corsage on my dress. When I reached my seat, tears were running down my face. She could not have known that my mother's name was Lily and that lilies of the valley bloomed outside my childhood home.

The sermon was on mothers in general. The fragrance of the corsage sent me back in time to my mother's garden. I was 11 and had just decided what I wanted to be when I grew up. "A missionary, Mama! I want to be a missionary in the wilds of Africa."

She smiled and hugged me. "You don't have to go that far to be a missionary," she said. "Let's take a walk." The walk around the block turned into a journey to another country as we passed familiar homes and I learned things I did not know.

"Mrs. Fontaine's arthritis makes it painful for her to do the simplest chores. You could clean her living room.... Mr. Schneider loves to read, but he is going blind. You read aloud well.... Mrs. Patel's husband has left her, and she has no extra money. You could watch her children so she could have some time alone."

For two weeks, I was a busy missionary until my art teacher introduced me to sunsets. I cloistered myself in my room with my easel and paints—while persons with a truer vocation for missionary work helped Mrs. Fontaine, read to Mr. Schneider, and watched Mrs. Patel's kids.

After church was over, I walked home, feeling that my mother was very much with me. In a trance of deep reflection, I stopped in front of Mrs. Devon's house. Mrs. Devon was a widow, and her children lived far away. I cannot take credit for my thought, for it came in my mother's voice, "Give Mrs. Devon my book."

When I got home, I wrapped the book in tissue paper while the soup was heating. I could not find a bow, but my corsage made the plain package beautiful.

God, we know you recognize that every person we lose is a gift to be treasured and a part of our hearts forever. Thank you for understanding that although we believe in eternal life, it hurts so much to lose someone we love. Comfort those of us who are grieving, Lord. Fill us with the knowledge that you are grieving with us. Carry us through this difficult time. Amen.

Polish our memories of loved ones laid to rest. Strengthen our resolve for going on without them...this would be a noble monument to their lives.

Blessed Creator, you have given us a heart with which to feel, but now my heart feels only despair and hopelessness. I miss my loved one dearly, and a cold and harsh wind blows through my soul. Bless me with a resilient heart and a renewed spirit, so that I can learn to love again without fear and without dread. Keep my faith steady and my vision sharp enough to see the good beyond the bad, the joy beyond the suffering, and the healing beyond the wound of the pain I feel.

God of all comfort, in the silence I hear your voice telling me that we are but bodies of light and love, forever transforming, never ceasing. And I know that although this person's body is gone, the spirit remains, eternal and infinite, and that I will never be alone.

The promise of eternal life dispels the fears of death. Knowing we will always be together in spirit gives peace to a heart that sees only earthly limitation.

Acknowledgments:
Publications International, Ltd., has made every effort to locate the owners of all copyrighted material to obtain permission to use the selections that appear in this book. Any errors or omissions are unintentional; corrections, if necessary, will be made in future editions.